for Butch

ESCAPING
ANXIETY

POWER IDEAS FOR

POSITIVE LIVING

*With appreciation for being my
golf "Manager" and my friend*

James E. Kilgore, Ph.D.

Escaping Anxiety

Power Ideas for Positive Living

2022© by James E. Kilgore, Ph.D.

All rights reserved. Published 2022.

BIBLE SCRIPTURES

of NavPress. All rights reserved. Represented by Tyndale House Publishers, Inc.

Scriptures marked (KJV) are taken from the KING JAMES VERSION (KJV): KING JAMES VERSION, public domain.

Printed in the United States of America
Spirit Media
www.spiritmedia.us

Spirit Media, and our logos are trademarks of Spirit Media

1249 Kildaire Farm Rd STE 112
Cary, NC 27511
(888) 800-3744

Religion & Spirituality | Christian Books & Bibles | Spiritual Growth
Paperback ISBN: 978-1-958304-08-2
Hardback ISBN: 978-1-958304-09-9
Audiobook ISBN: 978-1-958304-10-5
eBook ISBN: 978-1-958304-11-2
Library of Congress Control Number: 2022917725

SPIRIT MEDIA

REGISTER THIS NEW BOOK

Benefits of Registering*

- FREE replacements of lost or damaged books
- FREE audiobook—Get to the Point by Kevin White
- FREE information about new titles and other freebies

www.spiritmedia.us/register

*See our website for requirements and limitations

For my wife, Ruth, whose faith and love have helped me escape anxiety for over sixty-five years. We have proved that "perfect love casts out fear!

INTRODUCTION

Everyone who lives has some anxious moments. Some are devastating and have debilitating effects on daily living. Others are more subtle, and we tend to cope with them in a more constructive way. As a marriage and family therapist and a pastor for more than sixty-five years, I have listened to the struggles of those who feel anxious. This book is the result of discovering the ideas that transform our difficulties into discoveries.

We live in a world that often demands that we bow to the culture. That only feels like defeat. Discovering our transformation and overcoming cultural, family, and other demands moves us toward the powerful ideas that create positive change.

The cures for anxiety can be shortcuts. Medicine offers medications: for some those are necessary. Groups include pressures to conform to their mores and rituals: that sense of belonging can be helpful. Psychology offers ideas to guide us but we may fail to have the will to change our behavior. Only the transformational power of grace can bring real change.

We can be transformed only by a powerful change within us. As a teenager, I read a sermon by Thomas Chalmers called "The explosive power of a new affection." This book allows me to share with you new ideas, a new infatuation with powerful ideas to change your thinking and to explore some of the inhibiting boundaries of anxious living.

As you read these pages, may you taste some mental appetizers that entice your mind toward a deeper appreciation for spiritual discovery. I have been captured by Paul's admonition: "Be not conformed to this world! (Don't let the world squeeze you into its mold.) but be transformed by the renewing of your mind."

A transformed mind leads to a more satisfying day-by-day experience of the full potential of your life. May these power ideas create a foundation for positive living for you!

James E. Kilgore, Ph.D.

TABLE OF CONTENTS

SHORT STORIES OF HEART AND HOPE FROM ONE OF
AMERICA'S MOST BELOVED GRANDFATHERS

EXPLORING THE POWER IDEAS FOR ESCAPING ANXIETY

DISCOVERING POSITIVE WHOLENESS

SEASONAL LESSONS FOR LIVING

POSITIVE LIVING IN FAMILY AND MARRIAGE

TRANSFORMING THE MUNDANE TO THE MAGNIFICENT

EXPLORING THE POWER

IDEAS FOR ESCAPING

ANXIETY

POWER IDEA ONE

Delete Anxious Thinking

As I have listened to the news recently, I am more aware that so much of what government does is to create limits on the basic freedoms we enjoy. Those "unalienable rights" guaranteed in the Bill of Rights and the Constitution are shrinking. Through licenses and regulations, especially from Washington, we are being told what to do or say. Politicians proclaim freedom and "rights," but they result in limits on our lives. All of us are faced with a critical question. How can I create life without limits in the face of 545 people in Congress working every day to limit what I can do or say? It's a question we need to ask ourselves.

Living without limits is personal. The answers are not materialistic but spiritual. Too often we are looking for limitless life in all the wrong places. **This life is not the result of "luck."** I watched as a customer spent several dollars on lottery tickets. I don't think the government should be engaging in or regulating gambling. Too little of the money generated goes to education! If you want to *"waste"* your money doing that, you should be free to do so. The quest for happiness through what we have is always limiting. When Henry Ford was asked, "How much money does it take to satisfy a man?" he profoundly answered, "Just a little bit more!" The itch to have more is rarely ever scratched!

So what choices allow us limitless life?
I choose faith over fear!

Over forty years ago, a couple I had worked with in marriage counseling brought me a small gift. It was a framed plaque that read, "Fear knocked at the door. Faith answered. No one was there." Fear locks us in place and keeps the key to freedom. Healthy change only comes through faith in the possibility of change. Soren Kierkegaard, the Swiss psychiatrist, defined anxiety as "the alarming possibility of being able." Like the biblical brave boy, David, all of us face giants in our world and in our inner thoughts. To overcome them, we need to exercise our faith through the skills we have already developed. A small stone in a practiced sling shot brought down an enemy that terrorized a whole army of soldiers. All of us have faith; some use it more

16

effectively than others. Living in the prison of fear restricts our imaginations and our choices. Faith is the key that unlocks the prison cell.

I choose the positive over the negative!
I want to look forward, not backward.

Some years ago, I met Norman Vincent Peale, the author of the book *The Power of Positive Thinking.* Although he was then in his seventies, his mind was clear. Physically he lacked some of the energy he had demonstrated earlier in life. As we talked I was aware that he was planning the next year of his life. He wasn't looking back on what he had accomplished. It was exhilarating to be around him. Positive people are expectant people.

Life without limits is enhanced by our view of what lies ahead. As Satchel Paige, the aging Atlanta Braves pitcher, was fond of saying, "Don't look back; they may be catching up to you."

Whatever life may have brought you in the past, it is now only a memory. The joy of what lies ahead is what calls you to living without limits! Be pulled by your dreams instead of being pushed by your problems!

POWER IDEA 2

Be Open to Honesty

WHAT'S YOUR LEAD?

When a television news director determines the broadcast each day, he chooses a "lead story" be designed to capture the attention of the viewers and hold them throughout the broadcast. An author attempts the same thing in the first few lines of a book or story.

In today's television world, the lead is often about a fire, a murder, or unfortunately, a terrorist attack somewhere in the world. Occasionally, a warning of graphic pictures can accompany such a story.

Recently, a Christian grandmother confided that her granddaughter is gay. While she is making every effort to reassure her granddaughter that she is loved and accepted, the granddaughter's behavior is causing difficulties with other friends and acquaintances. The problem seems to be that her lead is "I'm gay." That confession might not be the most important introduction for some people she meets.

It reminds me that some of us seem to react to our limits, weaknesses, or problems as the first thing someone may wish to know about us. The opposite behavior is the way we wear social "masks," we hope will make us acceptable to others. If we are successful in hiding, we often feel isolated and alone. Presenting an issue as part of our introduction may cause us to feel justified when rejection appears to be the result.

The reason for examining this story is that all of us have a "lead" in our lives. What platform do you use when introducing yourself? Do you want to appear competent and in control? Perhaps you want to be treated as someone in need and ready for help. Do you have a part of your identity that is a "must accept" condition, such as this granddaughter projects? Is it working for you?

It reminded me that the New Testament writers also shared a "lead" about themselves. James described himself as "a servant of God and of the Lord Jesus Christ." Paul simply called himself "a prisoner of Jesus Christ."

Here's the question: What's your "lead?" How do you wish for people to identify you? Think about that.

POWER IDEA 3

Do Something You Value

WHAT ARE YOU ACHIEVING?

An interviewer stopped at a construction site to question the workers. He asked the first man who paused near him, "What are you doing?" The man replied, "I'm laying bricks." A second man came near, and the questioner asked, "What are you doing?" His answer was, "I'm making a living!" A third worker was stopped and when asked what he was doing, he paused and said, "I'm building a great cathedral."

All three workers gave legitimate answers, but there was a difference in how they viewed their work. I think we do the same today.

Some of us are doing monotonous tasks repeatedly, perhaps feeling bored with the activities of our daily lives. "I'm just a _____ (fill in the blank)" may be an expression of the absence of value about one's role in life. Without well-laid bricks, a building will be inferior or perhaps even dangerous, but the brick layer may not see the bigger picture of his work.

Making a living is certainly important for our families and meeting the obligations of daily existence. But we all know people who trudge through each day and go home to fall in bed and get up the next day to repeat the cycle. I recall a man in my counseling office who lamented, "I have climbed the ladder of success, but now that I've reached the top, I've discovered that the ladder was propped up against the wrong building." Even making a good or successful living may not satisfy the need for a deeper meaning in our souls.

How do we discover the "building a great cathedral" mentality?

Here are some suggestions:

> ***Don't get stuck in the small issues of each day.***
> A leadership speaker said, "Don't sweat the small stuff. It's all small stuff!" We certainly can't be satisfied with our work and daily contributions to our world if we dismiss everything as "small stuff" but we can be overwhelmed by the minutia of details.

Second, **value the things that are most important** in your life. Having a job and making a living for those I love is a value I never wish to lose. If I don't value what I do, it's likely no one else will either. A bright and outgoing young lady greeted her customers with a smile and was helpful to everyone who came in the shop where she worked. "You must really enjoy your work," an observer said. The young lady said, "I'm bored silly. I would rather be on the beach with my friends, but trying to be polite and helpful makes the time go faster until I get off and join them."

Third, **learn to be thankful for the place you have in life.** There are no menial tasks in cathedral building. Every job is important! It's too easy to sink into the despair of not accomplishing something important, but everything I do can become a part of a bigger picture. One note rightly sounded is important to the concert played on the piano.

I can only enjoy the things I value. To see life as including a greater purpose may give my life even more meaning. Jesus said, "I have come in order that you might have life – the life in all its fullness." (John 10:10 *Good News Bible*)

That accomplishment has blessed the entire world. How can I be part of that greater contribution? It's worth thinking about!

POWER IDEA 4

Discover Who You Are

FACING YOURSELF

One of the most frequent phrases I heard as a therapist was, "I'm trying to find myself." That usually indicates one is struggling with his identity. We see it in the question of gender identity and a marital crisis when a person questions his or her commitment to a relationship.

Integrity is founded on self-knowledge. A wise person summed up life's issues in these three questions:

1. Who am I?
2. Why am I here?
3. Where am I going?

The three subjects covered are identity (who), purpose (why), and destiny (where). These are questions we ask as we mature and develop a singular sense of personhood.

The issue is not new to our generation. In Jesus' stories about lost things: first, a sheep, then a coin, and finally a son recorded in Chapter 15 of the Gospel of Luke, human values are highlighted. The sheep reveals our attitudes toward possessions, the coin illustrates the importance of commitments to relationships, and the final story of the sons shows the loving heart of a father.

When the Jewish boy finds himself so hungry, he thinks of eating the pig's feed, there is an interesting verse in the text: it says "And when he came to himself..." (Luke 15:17, KJV). Then he realized he could go home to his father. There is the moment of truth for this young man. He knew who he was!

A number of years ago as I was in a training program, I attended a meeting of Alcoholics Anonymous. What I learned was that in order to speak, a person had to introduce himself as an alcoholic. "Hi, I'm Jim and I'm an alcoholic" was met by a chorus of "Welcome, Jim" from a group of fellow addicts. Admitting who I am is a start to solving my problems.

In the case of the prodigal son, the name we often give to Jesus' story, recalling where he had started out in life gave him courage to go home. I've met a lot of wanderers on the road back to the Father. In fact, when you come to yourself, that's the first step you want to take. If you haven't started toward home yet, the Father is waiting.

POWER IDEA 5

Let Go of the Past

LET THE PAST GO

Jesus said some things that seem very harsh out of context. For instance, a man said "I will follow you, but first let me go home and bury my father." Jesus' response was, "Follow Me; and let the dead bury their dead." (Matthew 8:22, KJV) Out of context, those words seem insensitive to a man's grief. In context the man was asking Jesus to wait for his father to die before committing to becoming a follower.

Today's invitations to follow Jesus are no less immediate. The New Testament emphasizes, "Now is the accepted time; behold, now is the day of salvation." (II Cor.6:2, KJV) But too often we wait for "the right time" to decide.

I spoke with a person who made a resolution to change something in his life. Three weeks later he has forgotten his vow. Why? The past had become a habit that he thought could not be changed. All of us get used to things the way they are and find it difficult to make or keep changes in our behavior or thinking. Let's examine those "limits."

The past is a major force because we don't like change! Like an old pair of shoes or a comfortable shirt, we stick with the familiar. Even when we know the thing we are "keeping" may be dangerous or harmful, we choose what is known rather than risk the possibility of a better unknown. It takes courage to change! But it can be done. Remember that the journey of a thousand miles begins with the first step.

For most of us, the "tapes" in our brains (perhaps we should say the CDs or MP3s now) have recordings of discouraging messages. Some are words of destructive criticism we heard from our parents as we grew up. Angry words spoken by a spouse in fights or divorces are played again and again in our minds. These echoes of the past are like chains that bind us to failure. We can't embrace the joy of the present because of the lingering memories of the past.

A friend shared how he helped another friend begin to "free himself" of his past. They each wrote down as many memories that had haunted them – the "sins of the past" for which they could not accept forgiveness. After some tears and confession to each other, they agreed to burn their lists of transgressions together. They read Isaiah's word, "Though your sins are as scarlet, they shall be as white as snow ..." (Isaiah 1:18, KJV) For some time to come, when they thought of the past, they reminded each other that the sins were "gone." Freedom began to grow and each of them found relief.

I love how children reason. A little boy learned in his Sunday School class that God forgives us and puts our sins behind His back. When he told his Dad what he had learned, the man asked sarcastically, "And what if God turns around, what then?" For a moment the little boy was stymied, but he finally answered, "Well, Daddy, I guess His back will still be behind Him." That's the wisdom and simple faith of a child!

Don't be pushed back to the past by your problems. Let this be a new day, and be pulled into the present by your dreams.

POWER IDEA 6

Eliminate Bitterness

MOVE OUT OF THE SPITE HOUSE

A friend sent me an interesting story about a "spite house." In 1882 a New York businessman – Joseph Richardson – owned a narrow strip of land on Lexington Avenue. It was 5 feet deep and 104 feet wide. Hyman Sarner owned a normal-sized lot adjacent to Richardson's skinny one. He wanted to build apartments fronting on Lexington, so he offered a small amount to buy the tiny lot which would block the view. His low offer insulted Richardson, and he demanded much more. Sarner refused, and Richardson slammed the door on him. Assuming the land would be available later, Sarner instructed his architect to design the apartment building with windows overlooking Richardson's land.

Richardson was infuriated and built his own apartment building to block the view. His building was 5 feet deep, 4 feet wide and 4 stories tall. On completion he and his wife moved in. Only one person at a time could ascend the stairs or pass through the hallway. Their dining table was only eighteen inches wide! The building was dubbed "the spite house." Richardson and his wife spent the last fourteen years of his life there. In 1915 it was torn down.

Revenge builds a lonely house with only room for one person! Richardson reduced his life to one goal: make someone miserable. He succeeded, but he and his wife were the victims. What a tragic but true story. Another old adage says we choose whether we want to become bitter or better.

The year is young and we have much time ahead of us. We don't have to build or live in a "spite house." It depends on the choices we make.

Revenge blocks our vision to other choices. When our feelings are hurt, we often decide there is only one way to deal with the circumstances – get even! Over the sixty years I listened to couples in the counseling office, I recognized that some spouses began to live to punish their partners, even if it meant they robbed themselves of happiness. Their bitterness robbed them of the opportunity to work for a better marriage. Divorce often occurred in such circumstances; two people leaving a relationship which might have improved. Others dropped the revenge motive and gave forgiveness in order to discover happiness together.

A declaration of "war" toward our enemies – personal or political - results in non-productive bitter actions. Some politicians get so angry at their opponents; they forget what challenged them to run for public service and begin to live to defeat – even to destroy – those who differ with them.

The Bible says "Get rid of all bitterness, rage and anger, brawling and slander, along with every form of malice." (Ephesians 4:31, GNT)

Holding on to our bitterness robs us of better options. A good place for our bitterness is on the altar of surrender. Leave it there! "Vengeance is mine; I will repay," says the Lord. (Romans 19:12, KJV) The wheels of that justice seem to move very slowly but always turn out right!

We have some choices—we can live in the lonely spite house—and suffer the limits of our bitterness. Or, we can move out and discover room to grow! I prefer that.

POWER IDEA 7

Make Your Foundation Strong

CHECK YOUR FOUNDATIONS

Some years ago, a neighbor discovered that she was having difficulty opening her windows and then that cracks were developing in a nearby wall. When she had a contractor look at it, she discovered that the room added to her house was built without a foundation. Of course, to have the problem corrected a new foundation had to be installed.

The Bible speaks to so many of the issues we deal with in our everyday lives. Jesus told a parable about wise and foolish builders. The foolish man built on sand and when the flood came, he lost his home. The wise builder by contrast built on a rock foundation and his house stood the test of the flood. Most of his hearers had either built homes or lived in one that allowed them to understand his parable. The description of foundations allowed Jesus to call for obedience to his teaching. "Whoever hears my words and obeys them is like a wise man," he said in this sermon. (Matthew 7:24, KJV)

Making wise choices for most of us does not come down to the foundations of our physical construction. The real measures of life, liberty and the pursuit of happiness hinge on the more important spiritual decisions of our lives.

How do we determine the truth which governs our behavior? Jesus said, "Do what I tell you." He didn't flinch from that instruction because, according to another passage, he is truth. (John 14:6, KJV) He embodies the laws of God, which result in positive blessings in our lives. Like Moses, Jesus instructed, if you don't pay attention, you will suffer the consequences. Build your house on a rock!

We cannot then say, like the relativists among us, "that's your truth; it's not mine." At some point a true standard for behavior and character must be set. Jesus said, "Build on the rock!" (Matthew 7:24-27, KJV)

So, my question for today is, on what foundation are you building your life? Multitudes of opinions exist, which are no stronger than sand. If you trust them as a foundation, your life investment can be destroyed very easily when the test of character comes. There is a rock of spiritual truth. I don't hesitate to point to the Scripture Jesus so often quoted. If you haven't discovered it, today would be a good day to see what the rock foundation sounds like and looks like. There's a storm-test just around the corner of life, make sure your living house stands!

POWER IDEA 8

Discover Reality

Writers are a complex group. Though many try, very few become wildly successful at the craft.

Ernest Hemingway was challenged to write a compelling story in six words. The challenger did not expect him to succeed, but after considering the task, Mr. Hemingway wrote: "For sale. Baby shoes. Never worn." Our enquiring minds write our own details around those words. A good story always stirs our own creativity. I imagine you have already been curious about what Hemingway had in mind.

I'm pushed to move in two directions. *First, is the greatest story ever written,* the story of God's love contained in the Bible, the best-selling book of all time! That simple story centers on God's love toward His creation. It is so clearly stated: "For God so loved the world that He gave His only Son that whosoever believes in Him might have eternal life." (John 3:16,

KJV). As the story unfolds, the events at the end of Jesus' life on earth demonstrate the completeness of that gift. As we move toward the death, burial and resurrection in the story, it becomes compelling in our reality.

The second direction that compels my attention is that the story impacts what I write in my actions every day. Yes, BOTH my life and yours become living stories that others read through our DAILY behavior. Like Hemingway – or Jesus – each of us will leave a story for others.

Unfortunately none of us know how long we have to write our story but each of us will leave one behind. Some may write words about us. One of my favorite lines a man wrote in the foreword of his book about his wife reads: *"She set her foot on the prairie and the wilderness became a home."*

As sobering as the reality is, each of us must give some thought to what we leave in our histories. "Lives of great men all remind us we may make our lives sublime; and departing, leave behind us, footprints on the sands of time."

The question we face today is, what story am I writing with my life today? Where is my creativity leading me?

POWER IDEA 9

Leave a Legacy

YOUR STORY IS WORTHWILE

A young man recently invited me to lunch. He wanted an interview about some historical perspectives on evangelical leadership over the years. I was happy to share with him. I walked away, however, thinking that too many of us have stories to tell that may be left in our memories as we age or fail to tell them. If we don't share them, no one may ever know the things we have learned, experienced or accomplished in our lives.

My wife has been working on scrapbooks for our children and writing her comments about pictures in the family albums. It is a painstaking task, but I believe, an important one.

Why don't we share our stories with others? Most often, it's because we don't believe they are important to anyone but us. Among the treasures I have are a couple of tapes (long before CD's or MP3's) of a conversation with my father before he died about the Kilgore history in Douglas County, Ga. I am glad to hear his voice and to add my memories each time I hear it.

A friend recorded for Ruth and me some copies of a weekly radio program we did in Southern California as well as some interviews I had as an author on television. They now become part of our story which our children and grandchildren may hear.

You don't need to be "famous" to have a story worth telling. In fact, God has created each of as unique creatures and has a plan for our lives. Someone will be happy to hear your story about God's blessings and how He has led your life. In fact, that story may have an impact on someone whose life will be changed because of what you shared.

Here's some suggestions: If you have the capacity, record some of your history, your life experiences, your marriage and family joys if they apply, and most of all how God has blessed and led you thus far in your life. If you don't have the capability to record it, then write one page at a time (maybe one page a day for a week … then a month. Lay it aside and then reread what you have written and edit and change to highlight what's important.

Like a will which says what you want done with your legacy of living, these memories may prove to be a lasting gift to a spouse, a child or a grandchild.

I'm always impressed when I read the Bible and learn from the stories Jesus told. Simple stories about the basic stuff of life are recorded in the Old and New Testaments. In one sense, we record our "soul" when we share what we have lived. Jesus said, "What is a man profited if he gains the whole world and loses his own soul." (Mark 8:37, KJV)

Most of the time you'll hear that verse applied to money or possessions. What I'm suggesting is that your soul – yes, your story – is a memory, a gift to give to those who follow you in life. It will be more important than numbers on an account statement if you can record who you are, whom you have loved and the people in whom you have invested your energy. Think about that!

POWER IDEA 10

Be an Encourager

GIVE A PLEASEANT FRAGRANCE TO LIFE

In South Korea I was speaking in a large church where my college friend, Dr. Billy Kim, was the pastor. My wife was introduced and said that Billy was a "sweet man." The translator paused a moment and then in Korean said, "She has said he is very sugary."

In another language words take on new meanings. When my grandson enjoys something, his commentary is "Sweet!" He really doesn't mean "sugary." I heard another man say, "It left a bad taste in my mouth." He was not talking about something he ate.

I began thinking about how our lives can be aromas to others. A co-worker in a youth program had a medical condition that caused her to have extreme body odor. Many people could not share a work assignment with her because of her condition. It was a great embarrassment for her. Fast forward to today and discover people who spread a life odor that drives others away from them. You can see it in their brutal "honesty" which causes pain for others. If we observe social interactions, we discover judgmental people who consider it their life mission to evaluate people around them.

But there are people you meet who make you feel you are in a rose garden. There is a pleasantness in these folks that creates a fragrance to life. You want to cultivate relationships with these uplifting people. What's the difference?

The people whose lives are like a fragrance put value into those with whom they interact. Do you have a friend who builds you up and makes you feel better about yourself? I think you may have discovered someone who is sharing the fragrance of life with those who are around them. You may also have encountered someone who causes you to think you have run into a skunk and the odor of the encounter stinks.

How do we choose to be "fragrance givers" rather than odor spreaders? The Bible speaks of those who are in the "triumphal procession in Christ" spreading "the fragrance of the knowledge" of God. Those who perish have "the smell of death." (II Corinthians 2:14-17, KJV). Check yourself out.

Fragrant lives spread integrity.

Having the strength to affirm others and make them feel good about themselves requires truly being honest with ourselves. Self-deceit is a destructive force in any life. The foundation of integrity is a true evaluation of our own strengths and weaknesses.

Fragrant lives shed positive affirmations of others.

Sometimes the fragrance comes through our own suffering. Like a flower petal that is crushed, each of us can share our strength in the face of difficult encounters and even false accusations. The result is an aroma of positive blessing to those around us. "Being crushed" may not be a sign of failure but instead a way to release the fragrance of strength and endurance within us.

Fragrant lives add something to the world around them.

Do you have friends that make you feel just a little stronger or perhaps see life a little clearer because you spend time with them? You probably have found a fragrance sharer.

Perhaps the more important question I must ask myself is: what am I spreading in the world around me? Is my life giving off an offensive odor? Am I willing to share the "fragrance" of what I've learned in a way that strengthens others?

If those around me grab a gas mask when I arrive, I should get the feedback. If they deeply inhale and smile, that also should tell me something about my life. What about you? An aroma or an odor?

POWER IDEA 11

Share Your Happiness

SHARE IT WITH OTHERS

Among the most common complaints a therapist hears is about "happiness." A single person is unhappy because he has not found the perfect mate – someone who will make him happy. A married person is unhappy because her spouse is not making her happy. The focus on someone or something outside yourself to bring you happiness will miss the mark every time. The danger in focusing on unhappiness is that we believe that happiness is an external treasure that we can discover in another person, in circumstances, or in some form of success.

May I share with you the secret to happiness? I've discovered it over more than sixty years in the counseling office. Here it is: **Happy people give others the gifts of happiness**. What are they? Attention, appreciation and affection!

Some adages may catch a part of the truth. One says happy people figure out what they enjoy doing and find a way to make a living doing it. That's good but still somewhat incomplete.

Another adage says happy people are those who have something to do and someone to share it. That's also partially true.

This is not an adage but a formula for happiness. All of us need three things to feel fulfilled in life: attention, appreciation and affection.

The first is attention: we want someone to listen to us. It begins in infancy when we learn to talk and we compete for the attention of our parents. Imbedded in that need is the focus on who we are and what we need. John Maxwell, the leadership guru, says: "People don't care what you know until they know that you care." If you have someone in your life who listens to you with focus, you are likely a happy person!

The second key word is appreciation. Is there someone in your life who values you? Happy people feel appreciated by others. They feel that significance of knowing that someone is grateful they are alive and a part of their world. It's a gift that can be conveyed at times by a word of encouragement, a knowing smile, or a gentle touch.

The third need is affection. Happy people feel loved. From the earliest moments of our lives we crave reassuring touches. We experience security when a mother affectionately cradles us to her breast. No matter how much we age, we never lose the joy of an intimate embrace.

This thought would be incomplete if I did not emphasize the deeper foundation of happiness. We discover it when we give away what we need. Happy people find ways to share attention, express appreciation, and give affection to those in their lives. When I give away what I need I receive as I give.

Two wise sentences catch this meaning:

"It is more blessed to give than to receive (Acts 20:35. KJV) and the wisest of all teachers said, "Do unto others as you would have them do to you." (Luke 6:31, KJV).

If you are looking for happiness, practice this formula and you'll discover it.

POWER IDEA 12

Learn to be Thankful

ARE YOU LIVING IN THE HOUSE
ON GRATITUDE STREET?

J. Ellsworth Kalas of Asbury Seminary wrote. "Some years ago, I bought a house on Gratitude Street, I can't say when I made the purchase, because this house was not like signing a conventional contract … But of this I am absolutely sure, that I never intend, ever again, to live anywhere else."

That author had perhaps caught the advice Paul gave: "Giving thanks always for all things unto God …" (Ephesians 5:20, KJV). That is an amazing prescription for living but not an easy one to practice. Most of us don't make our first words, thank you, when tough times confront us. Too often we complain that we don't understand. Why me? Why this? Why now? You know the drill. First, I'll complain and then maybe I'll understand and then possibly I'll be grateful. What do you think Professor Kalas learned about living on Gratitude Street that intrigued him so much? Try these insights:

First gratitude is a transforming factor.

Our instinctive reactions are anger, doubt, fear and blame. Gratitude calms us so that we can discover what is good in the circumstances and begin to overcome rather than to succumb to the elements that challenge us. Disappointments discourage us deeply. We discover too late that both people and events can disappoint us. When we react too quickly, we tend to "throw out the baby with the bath water." But if we stop to see all the elements in our disappointments, we can begin to concentrate on the things that are positive in our view rather than the dark clouds that seem to menace us.

Second, living on Gratitude Street opens the door to thanksgiving rather than complaining.

Listing our blessings and seeing the positive possibilities provides options for better and more rewarding behavior. Gratitude to God reminds us that He ultimately knows and provides all our needs. I don't have to worry when I know God is in charge.

A flight attendant woke the young boy who was asleep in first class and told him "we are experiencing turbulence; you'll need to put your seat belt on again." "Not to worry, Lady," the young said, "My Daddy is the pilot, and we'll be just fine."

Giving thanks to God reminds us of our priorities and restores our trust.

That can bring us peace in the face of most conflicts. A friend included this line in one of her devotional thoughts: "An attitude of gratitude can make your life a beatitude."

Transforming Trouble Street into Gratitude Street is a matter of perspective. We need never be afraid of trusting an unknown future to an all-knowing God. That's a good reason to be grateful.

POWER IDEAS

PART TWO:

DISCOVERING POSITIVE

WHOLENESS

POSITIVE WHOLENESS DISCOVERY 1

The Will of God

Many of us have asked this question. An answer might be the determining factor in choosing a career, like the ministry or other vocational direction. But most of us would like to be doing something fulfilling and hopefully believing we are pleasing to our Creator.

I find answers in the writings of those who have struggled with my questions before me. One such scholar was G. Campbell Morgan, a theologian and pastor of another era. When he was asked this question, he responded with three guidelines he always sought:

> **The will of God is never contrary to the clear instruction of the Scripture.**

His faith was in the precepts he understood to be guidelines for daily living. Obviously, the Ten Commandments include "Thou shalt not kill." Therefore, deliberately killing someone cannot be in the will of God!

Only a deranged person would claim, "God told me to kill him." That would be true of the other commandments as well. Preachers like to remind us that God gave Ten Commandments, not ten suggestions!

Morgan's **second guideline was the circumstances of one's life!**

As clearly as it would not be the will of God for me to rob a bank, it would certainly not include the purchase of something I really could not afford. A friend who had listened to a "prosperity gospel" preacher drove up to meet me in a luxury car and proudly announced, "God wanted me to have this car." Since he could not afford to pay his rent, I wondered. Paul's admonition was "My God shall supply all your need..." (Phil.4:19, KJV) but not necessarily your wants!

The third **guideline was the inner guidance of the Spirit of God.**

I don't think he meant a verbal instruction. Sometimes God leads us to see the needs of those around us clearly so that we may respond from the resources He has given us. Sometimes when we listen to a friend or a relative, we feel their struggle and reach out in compassion or empathy. God sometimes urges us to share another's burden at a particular point in our interaction. He "speaks" in many ways!

This week I ran across a very clear statement, "Always be joyful. Never stop praying. Be thankful in all circumstances, for this is the will of God for you who belong to Christ Jesus." (I Thessalonians 5:16-18, KJV) These are Paul's three instructions:

be joyful,
keep praying, and
give thanks.

Those are pretty straight-forward. I believe these guides can bring me a new understanding of God's will if I practice them. Let's make a commitment to do them each day of the year!

POSITIVE WHOLENESS DISCOVERY 2

Church: Event or Family

I recently read an interesting article which raised the question—is your church a family or an event? Since we live in a fractured and fighting world at so many levels, that seems like a good question. Think about your church when you try to understand the answer.

When people come together for a performance or to be entertained, the church is an **event.**

Too often, if the event does not hold the attention of all the members of the family or doesn't focus on perceived needs, that family or individual will seek other events. We refer to that on occasion as "church hopping". Some might even call it church "shopping." It almost sounds like seeing which department store carries your favorite items for purchase!

A number of years ago, a television program had as its theme line – "where everybody knows your name." Of course, the setting was a community bar! I wonder if we incorporate that kind of intimacy in our congregations?

Inside this question about the kind of church we seek is the role that our relationships play to each other. Because of that many organizations—not just churches—began to develop small groups where there is a greater emphasis on the value of the individual. It happens in the sports world. The larger team is a public value, but the team members become closer to each other as the "defensive unit" or "the offensive unit," in the case of a football team. In baseball the pitchers and catchers arrive early at spring training, not only for conditioning, but to build a sense of working together to win their ball games.

What does all this really have to do with the church you attend or belong to as a member? Here are three ideas:

The church bonds around a common faith. In the Christian churches, that faith is in the death and resurrection of Jesus. We share our faith in Him and that common understanding brings us together as one. Evangelicals take that belief outside their gatherings and seek to persuade others also to believe in Jesus. There is great unifying power in a common belief.

Churches at best add value to their members' lives by sharing a common fellowship. The greater the involvement in the friendship and comradery of the congregation, the more accepted and fulfilled the individual member becomes. The "family feel" draws us to return with regularity and to share in conversation and often in social times. The old saw is that church people can't get together without eating. Of course, when we get together for the "communion meal" instituted by Jesus, it adds a dimension like that to fellowship and worship.

I like the idea of the church as family rather than as event because **it implies a depth of belonging.** We have families which empower us and some which disappoint us, but there is a bond that draws us back to each other. We look to our families for identity and reassurance. Failing to get that affirmation in our families – that innermost circle - contributes to many mental health struggles in our lives. Discovering who we are has far more to do with our families than any other factor in our backgrounds. The church can then be a place where people can find true meaning and identity.

But only if we demonstrate the inclusiveness that Jesus described when He said, "Come to Me, all who labor and are heavy laden, and I will give you rest." Matthew 11:28, KJV)

Being the church in our world is a tall order. We can settle for giving people only performances and events. All of us need to find what it means to be the family of God!

POSITIVE WHOLENESS DISCOVERY 3

Heal Brokenness

The landscape of life is littered with a lot of broken things: broken hearts and broken relationships, broken dreams and broken people, broken bodies and broken promises. The list could go on. Disappointment is the result of our brokenness. When all we see is brokenness, then bitterness and despair set in.

Set that bleak outlook against Jesus dealing with a hungry crowd on the hillside and being given a lad's lunch of five loaves and two fish. He blessed and broke the loaves and fish into smaller pieces which turned out to be an all-you-can-eat experience and a collection of twelve take-home bags for His disciples. It was an amazing miracle one remembers when you stand beside the Sea of Galilee on a visit to the Holy Land.

We certainly live in a world of emptiness and despair, but Jesus' example may best show us how to deal with our problems too. Breaking the issues down and finding ways to share the responsibility of society's hurts is a doable process.

Government and agencies have tried to deal with deep issues with welfare and finances and have failed miserably. Without the element of compassion which the church brings to such issues, we cannot break cycles of despair and pain. When life has beaten you down, the direction to look is up!

When Jesus preached His sermon on that mountainside, He said, "Blessed are the peacemakers; for they shall be called the children of God." (Matthew 5:9, KJV) **Peace—within and without—can bring wholeness again.** Is that the answer for our churches, our communities, our schools, and our nation? Perhaps if we had more people aspiring to be peacemakers, we would discover fewer broken pieces and shattered people. Too often we are busier beating up those who disagree with us than finding ways to seek common directions of emotional and spiritual peace.

I wonder how many of us can join the peacemakers' club? We might be called children of God and discover ways to bring wholeness back to our world.

POSITIVE WHOLENESS DISCOVERY 4

Leave your Victim Behind

When you listen closely to people in a counseling office, you begin to hear common themes. Unless you are totally insensitive, the presenting problems sound very familiar. Whether they said it out loud or not, too many married people began by thinking, "Fix my spouse," and our problems will be over. If the problem is an individual struggle, the thought expressed was often "If only my circumstances were different." The common theme in many of our problems is that we believe we are the "victims."

The Bible illustrates that in many of its stories. Do you know Mary and Martha, the sisters of Lazarus, who often hosted Jesus when He was in Bethany? On one occasion Martha complained to Jesus to tell Mary to help her with preparations for the visit. She could have said, "Help—I'm the victim of a lazy sister." Another challenge to Jesus was a man who wanted his brother to share an inheritance with him in a more equitable way. He felt he was the victim of his brother's taking advantage of him.

These illustrations show us why we remain trapped in circumstances. Can you see it? We focus our attention on the other person or the circumstances. Sometimes we can't make any difference in either of these.

Here are some basic laws of bringing about change in relationships. They usually work to change circumstances too.

>The first is this: **I can ONLY change myself.**
>The second is: **I CANNOT change anyone else!**
>The third principle is: **if I change myself, my relationships will change.**

You will no longer be a victim when you liberate yourself from the prisons of your own thinking. In the holocaust of WW II, a German pastor was taken prisoner. He was being humiliated by the guards and stripped naked. Finally, one of the guards demanded his wedding ring, the last possession on his body. He later wrote, "They could take everything from me, except my sense of personhood." That insight allowed him to survive a horrible imprisonment. Few of us will suffer like that. He learned that no one could change him, but he could overcome brutality by holding on to the power of self-liberation. If that perspective worked in the most horrible of circumstances, it can be a game-changer where you and I live too.

Today you can be free of the shackles of your self-imposed prison by starting with your own thinking. Begin by acknowledging that you can only be responsible for who you are! The beauty of that insight is that it frees you from being responsible for any other person's attitudes or actions. When that truth changes you, everything around you will begin to change.

The Bible describes that change in these words, "Therefore, if anyone is in Christ, there is a new creation. The old has gone, the new has come!" (II Corinthians 5:17, Today's New International Version)

Genuine believers shed the old "victim" garments and start wearing the clothes of overcomer. Put your victory suit on today?

POSITIVE WHOLENESS DISCOVERY 5

Be Transformational

I belong to a United Methodist congregation. Unless you have had your head in a hole in the ground, you know that our denomination has gone through some struggles in recent months and years. As a result of the St. Louis conference, the "traditional" plan has been passed upholding the position of the Book of Discipline which states that homosexuality is not compatible with the Christian faith. It has caused much discussion among our churches.

The Apostle Paul must have faced similarly divisive issues with those who were part of the Church at Rome. He gave them this instruction in Romans: "Therefore, I urge you brothers and sisters, in view of God's mercy, to offer your bodies as living sacrifices, holy and pleasing to God - this is your proper worship as rational beings. Do not conform to the pattern of this world but be transformed by the renewing of your mind. Then you will be able to test and approve what God's will is – his good, pleasing and perfect will." (Chapter 12: 1-2; Today's New International Version)

The question for any congregation—or for that matter, any believer—is this: on what basis do we make decisions? Conforming to the pattern of the day or being transformed by the renewing truth of Scripture. Perhaps if we dig further into these two approaches, we will find clarity.

Conformity is the result of external pressure applied so as to bring about change. Each of us is faced with certain kinds of pressures. Often, we feel the expectations of those around us—neighbors, peers, family, and even the members of our church family. External pressure can become stifling to the point of emotional bondage. Obviously, that implies that something or someone outside of our thinking can impose their will on us. Such a pressure needs to be examined very closely to decide whether it is liberating or imprisoning. Paul's warning was: "do not conform to the pattern of this world."

Transforming, on the other hand, occurs from within. Just like a caterpillar becomes a butterfly through a radical transformation, a human mind gains insight and understanding. Obviously, Paul thought that instruction in spiritual truth would free us to prove what the will of God really is. Even the smallest of candles in a dark room creates a light by which we can see. So, the eternal light of Scripture sheds light and judgment on our behavior. That is transformation!

Jesus said He came to change people – that is, to call sinners to repentance. Only those who admit their need of a Savior will come. Those too proud to admit their need, won't. But the change from within is more than a reform of one's behavior; **it is the basis of a relationship that produces new insight and creates new character.**

Paul said it so simply yet magnificently: "Then you will be able to test and approve what God's will is – his good pleasing and perfect will." (Romans 12:2b, Today's New Int'l version). When we get together, we will be able to test and approve what God's will is – his good, pleasing and perfect will." No matter how we describe it, there is one factor determining what acceptable behavior is for believers: the unchanging Word of God, the Bible. May its truth transform us and lift us above the confines of today's cultural patterns!

POSITIVE WHOLENESS DISCOVERY 6

Chicken Soup for the Soul

I believe Jack Canfield coined the phrase "chicken soup for the soul." Of course, it was a play on one of the most useful things used to heal us when we are sick—chicken soup. I think Truett Cathy must have learned that secret before he created his now famous Chick-fil-A chicken sandwich. There's something about the sandwich and the soup that for many of us will fall into the category of "comfort foods."

I relate that to a habit I have each morning when I read from friends like Bob and Debbie Gass, David Jeremiah, and Charles Stanley. They all write devotional books which are like "comfort food" for my mind and soul. In them, I find meaning and understanding of the Scripture passages I read. Very often, the ideas shared in the Bible passage and the comments from these dear friends are just what I need for an issue I may be facing that day.

Many times, especially in moments that challenge my faith and sometimes cause me to stumble on the paths to my best in life, it is a word of Scripture or from one of these devotionals that gives me just the insight I need. Although I've read the Bible through a number of times, I almost always find new help the next time I read a passage with which I am already familiar.

I mentioned to another eighty-year-old how helpful my Bible reading habit was. He looked at me skeptically and said, almost sneeringly, "Yeah, right, Jim!" Although I was a bit taken back by his rudeness, I asked him simply. "Well, what is the chicken soup for your soul?" You might guess that he stared back at me, somewhat blankly and said, "I don't have one." I replied, "When you discover a better one than mine, please let me know."

So, my question for today, Friend, is this. Do you have some chicken soup for your soul? If not, today would be a good day to discover it!

POSITIVE WHOLENESS DISCOVERY 7

Discovering Healing

A number of years ago I sat with a mother who had raised a child with a disability. The child had just died as a result of the disease. She shared with me a reflection written by another mother about her experience. It's called "Welcome to Holland."

"I'm often asked to describe the experience of raising a child with a disability – to try to help people who have not shared that unique experience to understand it, to imagine how it would feel. It is like this…When you are going to have a baby, it's like planning a fabulous vacation trip – to Italy. You buy a bunch of guidebooks and make your wonderful plans: the Colosseum, the Michelangelo David, the gondolas in Venice. You might even learn some handy phrases in Italian. It's all very exciting.

After months of anticipation, the day finally arrives. You pack your bags and off you go. Several hours of flight and the plane is landing. The flight attendant says, "Welcome to Holland." "Holland," you say. "What do you mean Holland? I'm supposed to be in Italy. All my life I've dreamed of going to Italy." But there has been a change in the flight plan. You have landed in Holland, and you must stay.

The important thing is that they haven't taken you to a horrible place full of pestilence, famine and disease. It's just a different place. So, you must go out and buy new guidebooks and maybe learn a new language. You met a group of people you would never have known. It's just a different place – not as flashy as Italy, a little slower paced, but after you are there for a little while, you catch your breath. You look around and notice that Holland has windmills...and tulips. It even has Rembrandts.

Everyone you know is busy coming and going from Italy, bragging about what a great time they had there. And for the rest of your life, you will think, "Yes, I was supposed to go there. That's what I had planned. And the pain will never, ever, ever go away...because the loss of that dream is a very, very significant one. But if you spend your life mourning the fact that you didn't get to Italy, you may never be free to enjoy the every special, lovely things...about Holland." (Written by Emily Perl Kingsley)

I came across this article preparing for the funeral of Katie Frongillo, a Lake Arrowhead resident. I have never forgotten her or the beautiful lesson of these words.

I share them with you, dear reader, because you may have carried a heavy burden in your life. Or you may have gotten misdirected on your journey. It's never too late to accept where you are and discover a new perspective for today.

We can't always be responsible for the things that happen to us, but we can choose how we respond to them. One of the amazing lessons from the life of Jesus is that He did not want to die, but He chose the cross because of His love for us. As we leave the chill of winter behind and move to the warmth of spring, let us be grateful we do not have to live in the shadows of despair. We can choose to step into the light of blessing, even when we do not fully understand all events that have brought us to the choice!

POSITIVE WHOLENESS DISCOVERY 8

How Big is God

Theology can be difficult to understand at times. A youngster amazed his teacher when he said, "Me and God know everything!" "That's wonderful, Johnny; can you tell me how you were born?" the teacher asked. Barely pausing, Johnny said, "That's one that God knows!"

One of the least appreciated celebrations of the Church Year is Pentecost, the period of fifty days after the Resurrection of Jesus until the coming of the Holy Spirit to the followers of Christ. Every denomination includes some form of confessional statement about the Holy Spirit. That faith says that He lives within the person who acknowledges Christ as his lord.

When we lived in Southern California, a bass soloist named Bill Carle sang his signature song, "How big is God?" The question was answered in the lyrics, "He's big enough to rule His mighty universe but small enough to live within my heart." It was an unforgettable song.

I wonder how many of us know how big our God is. We don't pause at the "big enough to rule His mighty universe" as much as we wonder if God lives in us.

What an assuring thought that God can live in us!

It was J. B. Phillips who first asked, "Is your God too small?" Perhaps if we limit that Presence to what we know and what we can do in our diminutive capacities, then our god will be too small. However, this theology encourages us to believe that not only does God makes His presence known, but He empowers us through the vehicle of prayer.

Like Johnny, we may be able to confidently move ahead believing that God and prayer can accomplish the miraculous in our lives. **A universal quote says that you and God make a majority in any situation.**

We can easily be overcome with the problems we face in our lives, especially if we feel only our limited personal resources. But there is great strength in believing that our big God empowers us. As a friend whispered to me on one occasion, "Don't tell God how big your storm is; tell your storm how BIG your God is!"

That teaches me a lesson I can trust! Can you?

POSITIVE WHOLENESS DISCOVERY 9

Fear is our Enemy

For more than 18 years since the worst terrorist bombing in United States history, we have made claims that we cannot let terrorists control our lives or limit the freedom we can enjoy in our country. When events like the Super Bowl come to our area, we see the enormous preparation to guard against an attack on a major gathering for a sporting event.

After the bombings in England during World War II, Winston Churchill reminded the British nation, "We have nothing to fear but fear itself." Individually, we have very few options to control a terrorist attack, but are those the biggest fears we face? Too many of us have succumbed to the individual fears in our lives. How are you dealing with your fear? Here are two basic types with which we all struggle.

The first is the fear of being known.

This is the foundation of our wearing social masks. We hide who we really are so that people in our lives cannot know us as deeply as we know ourselves in the secret places of our being. We fear that anyone who knows us that well will not like us. At some level every one of us deals with a sense of inferiority. It can be a crippling fear.

A true friend is someone who knows us as we are and accepts us anyway. If you have such a friend, you are very fortunate. If you are such a friend to another, you are a priceless resource to them.

The second fear is more motivating.

Loneliness is the terminal illness of mankind. Each of us lives with the fear that we might succeed in living our whole lives and never letting anyone really get to know us deeply. To overcome that fear we reach out, risking rejection, in the hope that someone will accept us and want to be around us. To discover such intimacy is a singular reward in living. For many this is the motivation toward marriage.

Family is the place where we learn who we are.

Families with positive interaction breed more secure children who can cope with their fears. Where families do not function well, fears are heightened and can become debilitating. Allow the members of your family to share how they feel as well as what they think. Let your family be the place where there are no fears. Loving each other conquers fear, and everybody wins! Talk it over in your family. You may discover a breakthrough in communication.

It is not surprising when we think back over the angelic announcements from the New Testament that so many begin, **"Do not be afraid..."** (Luke1:10, NIV) God does NOT want you to live in fear. **If you master that lesson, you will begin living life without limits!**

POSITIVE WHOLENESS DISCOVERY 10

Forgiven to Forgive

Perhaps the most important word you may hear in a church is this one: *forgiveness*. It could be the most needed in today's culture. The Christian faith believes in GRACE. A Baptist evangelist said "grace" means "God's Riches at Christ's Expense!" Although it's a theological word, it conveys a psychological meaning as well. In so many venues—politics, the press, and in many of our relationships—our world tends to function around accusations and negative protests. Forgiveness includes relief from the guilt of our sins.

I attended a writer's conference some years ago where the audience was asked to vote for the best short story they had ever read. Much to the surprise of the leadership of the gathering, a large majority of those attending voted for a story Jesus told about a father who had two sons.

The 15th Chapter of the Gospel of Luke spells out the family dysfunctionality. The young boy insulted his father by asking for his final inheritance while his father was still alive! Then he went away from home and proved that he was not good at managing that inheritance. He took a menial job feeding hogs. Being hungry, he was tempted to eat some of the slop he fed the pigs, but an interesting moment occurs. He "came to himself" and decided to go home. Knowing he did not deserve to be forgiven for his behavior, he rehearsed his speech to his father on the way home. But the father ran toward him and offered him forgiveness for his rebellion and welcomed him home. His older brother could not bring himself to forgive his younger sibling.

Dealing with dysfunctional families and marriages for more than sixty years has made me aware that forgiving others is one of the most difficult things any of us can be asked to do. Family members and folks who once were friends can allow years to pass without speaking to each other because of unforgiven "offenses" that occurred. What a waste of time for both of the parties to such a circumstance.

A much more difficult reality is learning to forgive oneself. Too many of us feel that things we have done are "unforgivable." We inwardly punish ourselves and suffer because we cannot accept the past or the ways we have failed.

During the spring churches celebrate the resurrection of Jesus. Many people decide to go to a service during this season of the year. You don't have to go to church to find a quiet moment to ask for God's forgiveness. Like the father in Luke 15, He is waiting to welcome you home. The happiest day of my life began with a prayer, "Lord, I am a sinner. Please forgive me." He did!

That freedom has given me liberation for over sixty-eight years. God's forgiveness is real, and it can happen for you too.

POSITIVE WHOLENESS DISCOVERY 11

Lasting Support

One of the common phrases we hear in conversation these days goes something like this: "I've got your back!" I'm assuming most of us would understand that to mean the person who spoke those words would guard us from an unexpected attack from behind. A reporter described one of the President's lawyers as saying he would "take a bullet" for the President. That's an amazing commitment. It turned out not to be true!

It caused me to ask myself who might have my back. I'm blessed to have a wife of 65 years. I know I can count on her! But I also have some very special friends on whom I know I can count. I would include my three golf buddies who have become very special friends. I would also include a large number of people called the Pathfinders with whom I study the Bible on Sunday mornings at the First Methodist Church of Canton.

I pressed myself to think more deeply about the question, "Who's got your back?" I realized that the most important resource in my life is one that Jesus promised – not just to me, of course, but to all who trust Him. When He was facing death and gathered for the final time with His disciples, Jesus said, "I won't leave you like orphans. I will come back to you." (John14:18, CEV) "I will ask the Father, and He will give you another Helper, who will stay with you forever." (John 14:16, GNT). Those are the most reassuring words Jesus spoke to His disciples; and they become a reality for all who truly believe and trust in Him.

So who's got my back? The Advocate! He is called the Helper. I have the Presence of Christ, the peace of God and the power to serve. When Jesus promised the Holy Spirit, He said, "Let not your heart be troubled, neither let it be afraid." (John 14:27, KJV) He could have said, "I've got your back!"

Last Sunday, many churches celebrated Pentecost Sunday, the day we honor the coming of the Holy Spirit to begin the church on the fiftieth day after the resurrection of Jesus. I think next year I'm going to ask my pastor to call it "Got your back" Sunday!

POSITIVE WHOLENESS DISCOVERY 12

Our Greatest Power

I read an interesting line in a book written by a friend: "If it's too small for a prayer, it's not big enough to be a burden." Think about that for a moment. Even in our church circles we tend to place prayer at the foot of the list of options.

I heard someone say recently: we've tried everything else; we might as well pray. Oops! That's the place to start, not the place to end up.

I remember reading in my freshman literature class in college the famous words by Alfred Lord Tennyson: "More things are wrought by prayer than this world dreams of." He had the right perspective.

When Billy Graham was asked what the secret of his success in evangelism was, he quickly answered: "Three things—prayer, prayer, and prayer." That was not just a public answer. The main thing he shared with his team before every crusade gathering was prayer. I worked as a member of the New York team for the Madison Square Garden Crusade in 1957. One night I recall that he seemed especially burdened and asked all the team members to pray during the entire evening. When he gave the invitation, more than three thousand people responded to the front of the arena. It was a marvelous example of the power of prayer. He believed it was the answer to prayer, not his preaching, that brought results.

What is prayer? It is a conversation with God. It includes speaking and listening. Too often all we do is talk, asking God for what we want or need. But the listening part is also very important.

I remember an old Southern Bible teacher named Vance Havner who taught this truth: **God ALWAYS answers our prayers.** Sometimes He says "Yes." Other times He says, "No." And sometimes He says, "Not now." If you are a praying person, you no doubt have looked back on your life and been grateful God didn't answer all your prayers, "Yes."

You might have married the wrong person or taken the wrong job. Somewhere in that part of you called a "soul," you felt a "no" to that decision. Call it insight, conscience, or influence, but if you asked for guidance in prayer, let's call that prayer.

Here's an invitation. Pray each day for a week. **Try being grateful for the good things in your life.** Next, ask God for guidance in the things that may trouble you. Finally, pray for a friend whose needs may be greater than yours.

You won't change God's mind, but you may discover your attitude changes in the process. Yes, **"if it's too small for a prayer, it's not big enough to be a burden."**

Learn to Listen

His mother was at a loss. Her two-year-old had learned one word well, "No." It seemed that no matter what she said, he responded with his newly found refusal. The people around her in the store were divided. Some thought the little guy's defiance was cute; others looked like they wanted to spank him. His mother finally made him put down the toy and marched him out of the store while he yelled at the top of his lungs.

We have all witnessed a child taking advantage of a parent in a public place where one of the responses may be embarrassment.

When I went home after shopping, I read in a psalm some fascinating words from God: "But my people would not listen to me." (Psalm 81:11, KJV) Ouch, Israel was like the two-year-old in the toy store. And so are we at times. **We just don't listen!**

Do you wonder why people do not listen to God? Some are just too **independent** and self-willed. That seems to be the case of the angel named Lucifer who decided he wanted to be God before he got thrown out of heaven. Yes, human beings act in a similar fashion. As Flip Wilson said, "The Devil made me do it!" We don't need the Devil as an excuse. Most of us can express our defiance very well.

In the Old Testament, there are many stories that reflect the **indifference** of the people of Israel when it came to listening to God. Samuel, the prophet, felt rejected but God reminded him that when the people called for a king instead of a theocracy, the real rejection was of God! Indifference is also the most tragic sin in a human relationship. Over the years, husbands and wives can feel "taken for granted." One wife said to me, "He ignores me as if I was not in the same room with him." No wonder that feels so punitive and destructive in a marriage.

I learned early through my marriage and family therapy practice that it was not so much what I said that helped people bring about change in their lives. So often the key was that I really listened and then let them hear what they were saying about the problems they faced.

Listening and reflecting allows us to choose the changes we want in our behavior!

Perhaps the key question is, **what is God saying to us?** And are we really listening to Him? One of the ways we "hear" God speaking is through our eyes when we see another in need. When we dare to remain *insensitive* to the needs of those around us, we miss the call to service.

God always wants us to hear Him speaking to us. He whispers in our joys. He speaks in our struggles, but He shouts in our pain!

All we have to do is listen!

SEASONAL LESSONS
FOR LIVING

Here are some positive power thoughts for calendar
occasions and seasons of the year!

JANUARY

Approaching a New Year

ALERTS AND ANTICIPATION

New things bring changes to our habits. My car now has an alert system which tells me when I am drifting into another lane. My telephone holds all alerts until 7 AM before delivering them. The technology we live with can almost control us. But God has built into us a moral and spiritual alert system that is far more sophisticated—my conscience!

Deep within each of us there is an alert system which sends messages to our brains that remind us of the danger of drifting out of the lanes of good behavior. Alerts come when circumstances may be dangerous or people around us may be devious. These "protective" signals are summed up in the Ten Commandments and other documents. More intriguing is the compass that points out wrong directions from within my innermost being. These "laws" invite us to a fuller, more positive life!

When we stand at the door of a new year, we are also aware of a deep sense of anticipation. I can look forward to accomplishing new goals and exploring positive changes in my behavior. For many of us a sense of relief is experienced by leaving the failures behind us.

In fact the Bible instructs us to do so. In Paul's letter to the Philippians he says: "Forgetting the past and looking forward to what lies ahead, I press on to reach the end of the race..." These are very basic principles for living today.

First, **don't live life looking in the rear view mirror!** If you concentrate on just the mistakes you've made, you are looking in the wrong direction. Even if you are proud of the good things you've accomplished so far, your focus needs to be on new choices and opportunities rather than the limits of yesterday. One philosopher described it this way: "Today is the tomorrow we worried about yesterday."

Second, **the goal of the race is always ahead.** Almost every accomplishment is achieved one day at a time. The journey of a thousand miles always begins by taking the first step. Procrastinators seldom win the race as the old story about the rabbit and the turtle reminds us. Let today's distractions drop like an old garment. Wear the royal robe of forgetfulness and discover new liberty along your daily path.

Henry W. Longfellow wrote: "Lives of great men all remind us; we may make our lives divine; and departing leave behind us footprints in the sands of time." That only happens when we move forward and leave a direction to follow behind us.

As you begin a fresh year, raise your vision toward the future. Today really is the first day of the rest of your life. It is the only one you can change!

JANUARY

Welcome a New Year

WHAT DO YOU EXPECT IN THE NEW YEAR?

In her piece called "Resisting Christmas," Jennifer Hollberg implies that we expect too much for the season to deliver. The result is what she describes as "Christmas guilt." She concludes that "Things never change." She can only be right if we lower our expectations and hope for nothing more than we know.

The major resolution for many folks in a new year is to lose weight. That means crowded gyms and new exercise equipment that may last for a month or so in many cases. Then expectations are lowered or resolutions abandoned.

The Apostle Paul makes a staggering claim in the Corinthian letter: "If any man be in Christ, he is a new creature: old things are passed away; behold all things are become new." (II Cor.5:17, KJV) He is addressing

117

the spiritual change in conversion but we may learn something from the assertion.

Expectations change only when we no longer hold onto the past. You have to let go of what you had to gain what you want. The experiment with capturing monkeys begins with a bright shiny object in a bottle just big enough for the monkey to get his hand inside but not big enough for him to pull his hand out with the object in his grasp. So, the monkey holds on to the handful and loses his freedom in the process. Too many of us follow that pattern. We are not willing to give up the "security" of what we know to risk acquiring what might be a greater reward!

Expectations only become reality when we reach for something more. One of my favorite quotes is, "A man's reach should always exceed his grasp." Obviously that means letting go of something you already have to be willing to obtain something new. It works in our financial transactions, our areas of psychological growth, making new friendships, and other areas of change.

Oliver Wendell Holmes is credited with saying, "Most men see things that are, and ask why. I see things that could be, and ask, why not?" **There's the vision for new expectations!**

Open your eyes to new possibilities in this year. Risk a challenge you've never accepted before today. Discover that the reward of doing something is to have done it!

Happy New Year and happy discoveries as you grow through the coming year!

FEBRUARY

Discover Love

LEARNING TO LOVE

Be alert! The miracle to fulfill your dream may not be what you are expecting. It was easy to see why some people missed the Messiah at Bethlehem. He was not what they expected. Only a few found the promise in the birth of a baby; most of the world missed a miracle.

A life-changing miracle takes place for many of us when we discover that we are in love. Occasionally, someone will say, "I fell in love." But that really isn't true. We jump into love with both feet. Love is not an unrelated feeling, which overcomes a person in a magical way. Instead, love is a choice.

We choose to open our lives to someone and discover a rewarding experience. Hopefully we find that person to whom we open our lives is opening himself or herself to us; it becomes a mutually rewarding experience. These choices have different flash points.

One is chemistry. In romantic love there are moments of attraction, sometimes based purely on the physical appeal of the other person. Passion is often based only on chemistry or sexual attraction. But anyone who has been "in love" and had his heart broken knows that lasting love is far more than chemistry.

Another confirmation point in love is that emotional-metaphysical element. Deep sharing and values are often the foundation of friendships. Some lovers describe themselves as "soul mates" meaning they allow a deep connection of feeling and expression. A woman said to me, "If I think something, and he says it to me, how wonderful is that?" When commitment to sharing deeply occurs it forms a foundation for a lasting marriage.

The deepest level of all in a loving relationship is the spiritual one. The union of two souls is far deeper than the physical or psychological. The Bible describes that as "becoming one flesh." More than the union of two bodies, this involves the deepest "knowing" of another.

The Hebrew word "to know" is often used to describe the union of husband and wife.

Loving is ultimately the joy of continuing to discover who the beloved is. It requires rare courage to disclose one's self to another person. That is the definition of intimacy!

The Infant of Bethlehem was the ultimate in Divine risk-taking, allowing a young mother to "take care" of God! What a surprise to the world that was. When Jesus was named, the declaration "He will save his people from sin" was heard. His unassuming birth dares us to see God opening up to us and invites us to kneel at the manger to open our hearts to Him.

Isolation is destroyed when we dare to open to others. God opened to us in Bethlehem. He waits for our response.

FEBRUARY

Love's Secret

CAN I BE SURE I'M IN LOVE?

In my book, **LETTERS ON LIFE and LOVE,** I included a letter from a former patient who had remarried but was feeling uncertain about whether she really loved her husband. My answer is here:

Deep within each of us is the desire to love and the longing to be loved and accepted. This is your dream but in three attempts at marriage that dream has been shattered. Each time you reached out for love, it eluded you. Love was always there but never became a warm, living part of your relationships. Think with me about this.

What is love really? It certainly isn't something that walks up to us in another person's body! Of course we can be loved by others. When lasting love happens, we begin to feel it and see it first internally and then express it externally. We must learn to love and accept ourselves before we are free to accept love from another person. Only then can we give away true affection and care.

What you long for is to see a sparkle in your husband's eyes that says, "I want you." But you know that being sexually attracted is not enough. Love is more than fast breathing and physical excitement.

As a boy I watched my grandfather prune and graft trees. I think a loving marriage is like two trees being grafted together. Each can produce fruit independently, but when they are brought together through the uniting process, they now produce a new hybrid version of the fruit – a better quality than either of them could have produced alone. I'm not referring to children but to a quality of shared life.

When a couple loves each other, they do not limit or sap away each other's individuality. In fact one of the most important gifts we give each other is the freedom to grow in the life space that is ours alone. I recall a line that says, "At the heart of love there is a simple secret: the lover lets the beloved be free."

You seem to be waiting for love to happen to you. When I think about what you've said in the past, the picture I see is of a candle waiting for someone to strike a match and light it. You are like the candle crying out, "Why doesn't someone light me so that I can illuminate the room. I would make such a bright light." Being loved is more like a small flame or an ember glowing in the fire place. The relationship is the bellows which gently blows on the flame until it bursts into a more demanding and roaring fire. The bellows cannot create the flame; it must first be present. Your husband can't create the flame; he can only increase its passion as he expresses his feelings toward you. And you must do the same for him.

The real secret of love is in its direction. It is outgoing more than incoming. When I'm so busy caring about and reaching to the one I love, I have less time to worry about whether I am being loved. Concentrate on loving him deeply and richly; the result will be more than a surprise, it will be satisfying! What you can be sure of is your love for another person. You don't "fall in love; you jump in with both feet." Happy landing!

I wrote this letter to a real woman in 1977. I hope it offers hope and a challenge to each of my readers today.

MARCH

Experiencing Resurrection

Experiencing the Resurrection
Sitting in the Empty Tomb

About fifteen years ago I was leading a tour group through the Middle East and we were about to leave Israel on a Friday afternoon. An unusual set of circumstances made me decide to send my wife and the rest of the group with us home to Georgia and I returned to Jerusalem. After rendezvousing with another part of our group in the hotel, I found myself with no way to get a flight out of Israel until after the Sabbath day. Early the next morning I walked from the hotel through the streets of Jerusalem until I arrived at the Garden Tomb.

General Charles G. Gordon, a distinguished British officer, in 1867 came to Jerusalem and uncovered this tomb. He sent all of the ingredients in the tomb back to England and had them tested. There were no human remains in the leaves, debris and contents tested. Nearby is a rocky promontory which resembles a face. The Scriptures record that Jesus was crucified at the place of a skull, called Golgotha. In time this site has become known as Gordon's Calvary. The Garden, maintained by an English trust, is a quiet place for meditation and often a place where tourists celebrate communion together.

On this quiet Saturday morning, when the site had barely opened, I walked through the garden and went into the tomb and sat down. For almost an hour I meditated on Scripture and hymns about the life of Jesus, His death and resurrection. It was a life-enriching moment; I could sense the very presence of the Lord. When Resurrection Sunday arrives, I join fellow worshippers with the greeting, "The Lord is Risen" and if they greet me first, I respond, "He is risen indeed." Today those are not just liturgical words to be spoken on Easter morning; they are for me a statement not only of faith but also of personal reality.

Christians worship on Sunday to celebrate the resurrection of our Lord. Although I am just one voice,

I can tell you Christ is risen! An aged pastor was asked how he knew that Jesus was raised from the dead, and after a moment of reflection, he answered, "Well I know because I talked to Him this morning." Nothing changes life like a personal encounter with the living Christ. We join the company of the two travelling from Jerusalem to Emmaus and the disciples on the shore of Galilee and Paul on the road to Damascus.

Friend, I pray for you today that you will meet Him wherever you are and discover such a life changing experience. You too can sit in the empty tomb emotionally and spiritually and as the spiritual says, "Have a little talk with Jesus." May you have such a blessed Resurrection Sunday!

APRIL

A Renewal Rehearsal

SPRING IS HERE!

Spring's freshness yields to summer's heat and then to Fall's beauty to prepare for Winter's cold blast. The inevitability of change flows through nature.

In the psychological world and in our emotional lives we face change too. For some it is very threatening and difficult to face. We want to avoid the aging process. Our bodies change as they age. Children face the prospect of aging joyfully. Ask a child his age, and he will say "Nine and a half," emphasizing the half. Approaching sixteen and the possibility of a driver's license, the teenager keeps hope alive. But adults usually approach age differently. "How old are you?" is an inappropriate question to a woman. A man may say, "I'm *only* forty," meaning he still *feels* young. Later we think, "I'm not old; I just turned eighty."

But as age marches on, transitions are required. The Corinthians heard it from Paul: "When I was a child, I thought and spoke as a child, but when I became a man, I put away childish things." (I Corinthians 13:11, KJV) Every father who has picked up toys at the end of a day understands just a part of that statement!

If it is hard to grow up, it may be even harder to age gracefully. Some of us become bitter rather than better with the years. But a few develop a beauty to be admired and appreciated. Here are some hints for making older years count.

That famous theologian, George Burns, said: "Don't fall in love with your bed." He meant to get out and be active. Find a reason to go, do and share. The tennis court calls. The golf course beckons. A garden might be your possibility.

Explore your world and take the time to do the things you wish you had done when you were younger. I know those bus trips with "those old people" might not sound inviting, but you may find them stimulating and educational.

Find a cause to which you can commit yourself. Run for office, support an organization, plug into a congregation, or find a child who needs a friend.

Finally, share the things you've learned with others when you have an opportunity. Help with a career day in a local high school or volunteer as a mentor.

If you are fortunate to have a grandchild close by, remember that you may be the very best resource for understanding acceptance and love that child has. Don't miss your opportunity. It's OK to spoil them just a little bit!

Above all, don't forget that this life is but a rehearsal for the eternal one. There's another world waiting. The little girl told her pastor she knew what the Bible was all about. "Tell me," he said. "It's <u>B</u>asic <u>I</u>nstructions <u>B</u>efore <u>L</u>eaving <u>E</u>arth," she beamed.

A little child will lead us.

MAY

My Mother's Christ

A LIVING TRIBUTE TO MY MOTHER

Dear Mom:

After forty years of living together, I thought it was time to reflect on what it means to be a son, particularly your son. Let me begin by saying "thank you" for some of the things very special about you.

Thank you for being intellectually curious. I'm glad to be the son of a woman who did not check her brain in at the hospital in exchange for her baby. I am sure that one of the reasons I am an insatiably curious person, a persistent reader, and an expressive writer is because you talked to me so much as a child. It is a joke that is still going on with your grandchildren that you are "generally speaking" around the house. That exposure to books and ideas, to people I could openly encounter and to educational opportunities is a priceless heritage. It has shaped much of my development as a person and as a parent.

Thank you for not being possessive. You never really pulled the emotional umbilical cord. I'm sure it was difficult for you to see me traveling very early to other states and leaving home to attend a resident high school in the 8th grade. I know it was hard to see me move all the way across the country when I married. The fact that you knew how to let your children go became more evident when my sister went to South America. Only when I think about my own children leaving home can I appreciate the red eyes I saw the mornings we left home and the tears you often shed in airports. Thank you for enduring the pain and not making me feel guilty when the urge to explore life found its wings in my experience.

Thank you too for growing with me. It's hard to be a mother at age 17. You must have struggled with that responsibility. You always had a knack for using your resources well. One of those resources was your own parents. You gave me something very special by allowing me to experience their love and care when I was very young. While you could have tried to teach me everything, you were wise enough to use many people, including my grandparents to help shape me in the early days of my life. That was a wise choice for which I can never fully repay you.

Thank you for having an "open home," not only to your friends but also to mine. You and Dad brought some truly great people into our home who have deeply influenced my life. It was always easy to invite my friends to come home for dinner or to spend the weekend. I never remember your saying that it would be too much trouble or that you were too tired. I only remember having the kind of home where my friends were always welcome. The memory bank of meals we shared with visitors is an immeasurable treasure. My interest in the world was sparked by missionaries from so many countries who told about their parts of the world while we sat around the dinner table. I have since learned that not only did they "rub off" on us but also that we shared a very special family life that was contagious to others.

Thank you for helping me know what to choose in a wife. Maybe I should just be thanking Dad for marrying you. You never sat down and said, "This is the kind of girl," but your ideas guided me as did the relationship you and Dad modeled for me. I somehow knew that a good marriage was made up of open exchanges, managing differences and an ever-presence expression of care and concern.

Above all, you have been a Christian mother. I don't want to excuse your frailties. You haven't always been right, but you've always been there when the crises of life occurred. From the time you met Christ when I was twelve, there was a difference in your life. It became more visible over the years. I wrote this poem in 1963, but it still expresses many of my feelings about your sharing Christ with me:

My Mother's Christ

When I was but a little lad, my mother told me
of Him Who, though good, died for the bad.
She told me that He loved them.
And she would come and sit by me
and tell me of His fame.
I thought she was old fashioned
and that her Christ was too.
I could scarcely have imagined
that all of this was true.
I waited for the day to come
when I would be of age,
And leave my Mother's home to star

on this world's stage!
I would pay the winner's price
for my mark on history's page.
But I met Him one day in a quiet place.
There I knelt to claim His saving grace.
And through the years we walk
in perfect harmony
And through the day we talk,
my Mother's Christ and me.
I often think where I might be
if Mother hadn't shared
The message of her Christ with me
and told me that He cared.

Let me close my letter by **thanking you for being a good grandmother.** I've watched you with my children, your grandchildren and have seen again many of those things that I experienced as a child.

One Christmas, as we sat together opening packages, one of the special insights of that holy season reached out and grabbed me. God wanted His son to know what it was like to have a mother. Thank you for showing me what it means to have a mother.

Lovingly, Jim

This is an actual letter and poem I wrote my mother in December,1976. She died in June,1997. It was later included in my book, LETTERS ON LIFE AND LOVE (Harvest House, 1978).

MAY

A Tribute to Family Sacrifice

"He was just a kid." A sad sentiment to be spoken about a barely twenty-year old brought home in a flag draped coffin to a small Southern city. The veterans stood proudly at attention and saluted as the casket passed. Some wiped a tear from their eyes.

Like so many young men in his hometown, this was the boy you would want for your son. He never forgot to say, "thank you." To those who were older, he always responded, "Yes, M'am" or "No, sir." He had learned all the lessons his father and mother taught him, including that sense of bravery and patriotism that led him to sign up for service in the United States Marines.

He was well trained and fiercely proud of his unit. When they were called up to Iraq, he was ready to do his job. He was a Marine, brave and fearless! After only a few months in the battle zone, he was killed in a surprise attack.

"He was just a boy," his mother sobbed. The assigned Marine knelt in front of her and gently placed the folded flag in her lap. Her husband's arm was around her side, but he too wept for the loss of his son. "Your son was a hero, M'am," the marine officer said to her. "His country is proud of him and mourns his loss with you."

War turns kids into heroes. From the hell of battle, they are welcomed home to the mansions of the Lord. These heroes—not the political pundits or the press – keep us free. Let us not forget that our freedom is not free. The blood of our heroes has bought it.

As we celebrate Memorial Day, let us take time to thank the families of those who have given their sons and daughters in wars past and present for their sacrifices. Nations have heroes; America pauses to remember ours and to thank those still living. Families too have heroes. When we remember and honor them, we reinforce the ideals that tie us more closely to each other—our faith, our freedom, and our future! God bless all the families of veterans!

JUNE

Lessons from My Father

A LETTER TO MY FATHER

Dear Dad:

This is a letter I wanted to write while you were alive, but it's never too late to say things that are true. Thank you for being my Dad. I realize I learned so much from you.

I learned the quiet confidence of a man who knew what he wanted. It showed in your sales work. People trusted you and you did not let them down. You modeled for me what it meant to keep your promises. I'll always be grateful for that lesson.

I learned generosity from you. I watched you open your wallet and your heart to those in need. **Thank you for teaching me the joy of giving.**

I watched you love my mother. You accepted her as she was and encouraged her to grow. She was a beautiful teenager when you married, but after sixty-two years of being loved by you, she became a capable and wonderful woman. You loved my little sister too, but Mom was never threatened because she was always first in your heart. You taught me how to be a grandfather too. Watching you bait a hook or teaching a grandchild how to drive, you always seemed to say, "This is what love looks like."

Most importantly, you taught me about the heavenly Father. I can pray now because I heard you talk to your Father.

It's Father's Day. I could go stand at your grave and meditate quietly. I chose instead to share this letter with my friends. Maybe we'll all be better fathers too.

Love, Jim

In memory of Woodard E. "Woody" Kilgore, 1909-1995

JULY

Family and the Fourth

My brother-in-love was an immigrant. In 1968 when my sister returned to the United States after her first term as a missionary in South America, she brought home her fiancé – an Ecuadoran physician.

Like many families, my parents had some reservations about her marrying someone from a different country, particularly what that would mean about their visits with future grandchildren. You can imagine that it was difficult for them to hear about the birth of their grandchildren in Ecuador while the rest of the family was here. Doors of opportunity opened for Dr. Cabascango and soon they had a residency in this country.

In 1995 Dr. Cabascango stood with a number of men and women in Miami, FL at an impressive ceremony where new citizens are welcomed into our country. He earned my respect as a family member, a physician and as an informed citizen.

I feel sad for those people who do not learn what being an American means through the legal process of becoming a citizen. Not only does it mean gaining knowledge about our history and our laws as a nation but also usually includes learning to speak English and acquiring the skills to assimilate into this country. This identification has been diluted.

What does it mean to be an American? More than just being born into one of our fifty states, Americans identify with a certain hope for mankind. Our Declaration of Independence says, "We hold these truths to be self-evident, that all men are created equal, that they are endowed by their Creator with certain unalienable rights, which among these are Life, Liberty and the Pursuit of Happiness."

In recent years the word "rights" has taken a more encompassing meaning. Much of what the Constitution addresses has to do with legal and voting rights under the law. It does not guarantee protection for behavioral choices or preferences.

Most of the amendments keep the Congress from interfering or regulating the practice of religion, from prohibiting a citizen's right to bear arms or from being forced to house soldiers in one's home. Later actions abolished slavery and gave women the right to vote. It is clear the Constitution intends to protect us from government and reacted to the excesses our forefathers had experienced in the forms of tyranny.

The Declaration of Independence clearly delineates the freedom to be born (the right to life), the freedom to have opportunity (liberty) and the freedom to work to fulfill your personal dreams (the pursuit of happiness). Our family was enriched by sharing these goals with someone from another culture and nation before he died in 2016.

As we wish our nation another birthday, let us resolve to rediscover and reassert the hope and the qualities that have made us the envy of the world.

President Herbert Hoover said it well: It is those moral and spiritual qualities which rise alone in free men, which fulfill the meaning of the word 'American.' And with them will come centuries of further greatness for our country." (August 10, 1948)

Happy Birthday, America, and may each of our families be encouraged to live out this American dream!

DECEMBER

Jesus' Grandmother

When Jesus' Grandmother
Taught Sunday School

One of the favorite things that happens at Christmas is seeing people you haven't seen in a while and remembering experiences you've had together. As a retired minister one of my joys is to have someone recall a story I told during the season. It happened the other day.

One family was not in the church going habit, but the neighbors invited him to come to Sunday School with them and his parents gave permission. He came home telling his parents about what fun he had at the church. "Who was your teacher?" his mother asked. "Jesus' grandmother," the young man answered. "What makes you think that, son?" his mother asked again. "Well, all she did was talk about Jesus; so, I guess she was his grandmother!" Every grandparent can appreciate his joyful explanation!

It's the time of year when we decorate and go to parties and give gifts to each other. Perhaps we even get around to thinking about the reason for the season – the birth of Jesus. When we do our hearts fill with joy and gratitude for what that birth and His life have meant to history. We recall our years B.C. (Before Christ) and A.D. (in the year of our Lord).

Bethlehem – the city of Jesus birth – was where the warrior king of Israel, David, was born. Not only is it a special city – even today – but it remains a hallowed spot for the Christian world. We may not get to go physically to Bethlehem this year, but in our hearts, we can join shepherds and animals in our curiosity to sense the meaning of that unusual birth in a stable. As they did in days of old, wise men still seek Him. They brought Him gifts and we can too.

All the Christ Child seeks from you and me today is the gift of worship, whether in a church or on a battlefield. In an inexplicable experience we can proclaim Jesus Lord by symbolically giving Him our hearts. Jesus is the reason for the season. Find Him, worship Him and try being his "grandmother" by sharing that good news with those you meet! Think about that!

DECEMBER

Coping with Grief at Christmas

She was a young woman, more attractive than many. I spoke to her after the funeral. Through those tear-stained cheeks, she looked up and asked, "How do you fill a hole in your heart?" Her question was one I included in my book, LETTERS ON LIFE AND LOVE, some years later.

Grief is a devastating emotion. In many ways it is like having a "hole" shot through your heart. Pain is always part of our first reaction, mixed with a sense of loss and a stunned feeling of unbelief. After the first shock settles, guilt often follows; then anger. Finally, reality shames us out of our self-pity into a new course of action.

A suggestion for filling the void in your life is to start by experiencing *good* grief. Don't deny yourself the right to feel anything, whatever it is. Feelings in themselves are neither right nor wrong. Behavior can be judged; our feelings simply exist.

The first temptation is to block the feelings you may think are offensive to your own judgment or the opinions of others. It is irrational to believe we can avoid our unacceptable feelings and self-responsibilities. Whatever we deny and attempt to store in our inner being can unfortunately erupt at unpredictable moments in our life cycle. So, go ahead and grieve – get all your feelings out.

When someone we love, especially a spouse, dies, our feelings won't all make sense. Relief that the person is no longer suffering can be over-ridden by anger that you may be left alone for the rest of your life. Some days you'll feel remorse for things you wish you had said before your spouse died. On other occasions you will discover something that person wrote or a gift that recalls a special time of joy you shared. The loneliness you experience may feel overbearing.

Don't fall into the trap of self-pity. Feeling sorry for yourself is wasted energy. You won't appreciate your sympathy, and no one else is around to commend you for it! Carl Sandburg wrote: "Life is like an onion; you peel one layer at a time, and sometimes you weep." Tears are disconcerting at times, but they assure us that we are neither pain less nor dead. Weep when you must, but not for the benefit of others.

I was driving and saw a truck passing on the other side of the street. Its cement company slogan was "Find a hole and fill it!" A bit of a pun, but it contains the truth. Out of opening ourselves to pain in our own lives, we often discover the strength to communicate understanding to others. When you find a hole in someone else's heart and help them fill it, you will discover again the joy of giving. The only love we keep is the love we give away. Think about that!

DECEMBER

Dog with Us

The little boy was just learning to read. He did his best but his yet undisclosed dyslexia caused him to see the word backwards. He was trying to read Isaiah who said, "God with us!" It is a familiar phrase at the Christmas season.

Hearing this mistake reminded me of the dogs I've known at Christmas. When I was a boy, we had an old hound dog. If I sat down, he would come where I was and put his head in my lap to be petted. I guess I experienced "dog with us."

A good friend shared an insight about his dog that had grown old, nearly blind and pretty deaf. He would crawl into the bed at night and pat his owner on the leg. In earlier days that was a sign the dog needed to go out, but toward the end of his life, he simply wanted to know that his master was still there.

Another thought came to mind as I pondered "dog with us." A country doctor came to visit an elderly patient at his home. As the doctor sat next to the dying man's bed, the patient asked if he could tell him what dying would be like. The doctor paused a moment before answering, but in that moment his dog had gotten out of the car and was scratching at the patient's door. The doctor said, "My dog doesn't know what else is in this room, but he knows I'm in here. I don't know what else is in eternity, but I do know that Jesus is there. That's enough for me."

What do these dog stories have to do with Christmas? Maybe they can teach us some of the realities of the season. In the dark moments of life, like the dog patting his master's leg, we are not trying to go away but to be reassured that our Master is still there. Isaiah answered the anxious moments of our lives 700 hundred years before the birth of Christ. Read the words correctly, "God with us!"

Eternity is something of a mystery to all of us. The doctor's dog reminds us we have nothing to fear because we have Jesus' promise: "Where I am, there you will be also." It doesn't really matter what's behind the door when we know Who is behind it.

The Christmas story has so many mysteries: an old priest's wife is unexplainably pregnant (John the Baptist), the Virgin Mary has a baby boy (Jesus), a new star appears in the sky, and shepherds hear angels singing in the night. But when you are close to your Master, you hear the words, "Fear not … it's good news!"

A friend reminds me that God spelled backwards is dog. Who knows that when we pay attention to our dogs, we might just learn some special lessons about God. Christmas is almost here. Pay attention to your dog; he may point you toward God. Merry Christmas to all and a good night!

POSITIVE LIVING IN FAMILY AND MARRIAGE

Lessons from Grandparents

WHAT I LEARNED FROM MY GRANDPARENTS AND NEVER WANT TO FORGET!

Today, if you are a grandparent, you may need to learn something about computers or cell phones from your grandchildren. I have. But I am fortunate to have learned a number of significant lessons from my grandparents. Several of them I want to teach my grandchildren and I never want to forget them. Here are five I'll share with you today:

First, keep your life as simple as you can. The world is complicated enough, but family life can be an oasis in the desert of calamity. Take time to listen to the stories of your past and the things your grandparents enjoyed or endured. I'll never forget some of the stories my grandparents told me about me - and especially those they told me about my parents. Your family history may not be important to anyone else except you. Remember that when your grandparents are gone, they will not be able to share those memories with you.

Second, my grandparents taught me to handle money wisely. Two lessons were most essential - know how much you have and don't overspend. Budgeting is a base line in most financial systems; they called it "prudent spending." Their frugality kept them from spending more than they had to on any item. Sometimes they traded things and other times they saved a little longer until they could pay cash. Besides, plastic was not as frequently used then. They took pride in regular savings and earning the best interest they could. If the love of money is a root of much evil, they believed that the wise use of money was a course of great benefit. It is a great lesson to remember.

Third, my grandparents believed that nothing beats a home-cooked meal. I'm not sure it was always the food that was important. Perhaps it was simply being across the table from folks you loved and keeping in touch with what was happening in their lives. The dining table was a center for building strong family bonds.

Fourth, they believed that a little elbow grease never hurt anyone. They modeled hard work and enjoying their success from it. A vacation always seemed important but they were happy to get back into the rewarding routine of their lives.

Finally, they taught me that the unseen things in life are often the most important. They made time for worship and witness to their faith in God. Remember the Source of your blessings! That was more than a cliché to them. At meals they bowed their heads and held hands in gratitude. Food always tasted better after giving thanks for it.

They spoke few words but taught volumes. I hope I do as well in teaching my grandchildren.

The Family Value Table

WHAT ARE YOUR FAMILY VALUES?

The Month of May has been traditionally designated as "Family Month." Perhaps the major cause is the presence of Mother's Day, usually the second Sunday of the month.

Having spent more than five decades treating marriage and family problems, I remember that. Family is very important to me and I still want to help families discover and maintain their values. We live in a time where almost all traditional values are being challenged. It is true of our families too.

The world has many voices crying out to set the value table at your household—social groups, political leaders, educational organizations, and the church. However well-intended they may be, the responsibility of defining and educating our children falls squarely on the shoulders of parents. Upon what foundation will my children educate their descendants?

May I suggest a starting place?

Value education begins with the truth of sacred Scripture. "In the beginning God … created." (Genesis 1:1, KJV)

A Divine plan containing male and female aspects underlies the institution of marriage and family. Existing for centuries before our preferences and diversities, a clear pattern of male-female interchange is reflected throughout all societies. Families who begin here to teach marriage values give their children a universal truth rather than situational pleasure as the bed rock of life!

In the crucible of marriage is the possibility of commitment that teaches a child to trust the parents who brought him into existence and the shared ability they use to guide him toward hopeful reality in the world. That courageous trust allows an exploration of values and concerns on the foundation of solid teaching.

Values are modeled for our children as we live out the realities of our lives. In this context a child may ask questions without fear and receive honest answers to his inquiries. No parent need fear that process. Our living witness to the values we espouse provides the most powerful, if not always the most eloquent, answer as to why we live as we do.

When values you believe are rooted in truth, your child will discover a solid foundation on which to develop his thinking and faith. That child will undoubtedly choose his parents' loving admonition over those of any purveyor of other values.

So here are your questions: **who determines your family values**? And who is teaching them to your children? These are the questions parents must answer.

The Face of the Future

BUILDING STRONG CHILDREN

No one doubts that our children will inherit what we leave them. Some children will inherit money and may exhaust its potential very quickly. Parents leave wealth but may not instruct about its use. Other children grow up in poverty but become wealthy because their parents taught them character and determination. If the present is a reflection of what our parents gave us, we must seriously ask what will the face of the future look like, especially if we judge it by what we are giving our children now.

A great preacher once wrote, "When times are troubled, we ask God to give us men to match our mountains." In response God gives us children and says, "Here is the building material." If these are our building blocks, what are the instructions that direct their outcome? Here are some basics:

For years Truett Cathy, founder of Chick-fil-A, taught a Sunday School class for young boys. He said, "It's better to build boys than to mend men." The lesson is: **children are to be taught carefully.** What we believe and what we teach our children does matter. If we don't teach them how to use money, they will be financially bereft. If we fail to teach our children values, someone else will impress their thinking on them. If we do not teach them to respect authority, our children will rebel against all demands placed on them. If we don't teach them how to make good decisions, they will be easy prey for the human vultures of the world. They will learn the virtues of hard work and its rewards from us.

Words alone are not enough. **Parents have the privilege of modeling what they profess verbally.** When we face our problems with courage, they see a model for coping with life. If we accept responsibility for our failures, our children learn to face honestly their choices and their consequences. When we discipline them for bad behavior, they learn that everything produces results – good or bad. If a parent whines and complains about his lot in life, can he expect anything but a "victim" mentality from his children?

Sharing honestly with our children is the key to building lasting relationships. Truthful parents raise inquisitive children with open minds and open hearts. Nothing hinders a child's trust and desire for intimate sharing with a parent than dishonest or hidden behavior. As an infant a child does what we say. As he matures he learns to choose for himself. As an adult he chooses whether he will be an adult friend to his parents. If you have shared with him as he grew up, he will want to share with you as you age together. If you shut him out when he is young, he will return the favor when he becomes an adult.

The greatest joy of parenting is unconditional love. Watching my granddaughter demonstrate her love for my great grandson has provided a perspective of the years. Unconditional love never spoils a child. Conditional love can cripple him for life. Something a child does can be described as bad, but a child is not bad. The Scottish poet, Robert Burns, said: "Home is the place when you have to go there, they have to take you in." How much better for a child to learn that no matter what happens in life or whatever failure he may experience, there's always a parent who loves him and is waiting to hear from him.

Four suggestions for today:
>   teach carefully,
>   model consistently,
>   share honestly and
>   love unconditionally.

What your children inherit will give them strength to face their mountains and will make them the shining face of the future.

What Makes a Strong Family

ONE YOU CAN HAVE TODAY

That's a question I have been asked many times in my work as a marriage and family therapist. Far fewer research and studies exist about happy families than about sick ones, but four characteristics emerge from all the findings available. Here they are:

The members of a strong family appreciate each other. They contribute to making each other feel important and worthwhile. More than any other group the family determines who we are and how we feel about ourselves. Your family's appreciation becomes the single most important contribution to a healthy self-image. That means too that your acceptance of your family is extremely important.

Strong families communicate. They talk to each other! The conversations include the conflicts as well as the pleasant times they share. Each member feels that it is acceptable for him to talk about his feelings and ideas within the family without fear of condemnation. Communication between members of the family is essential to the good mental health of each member of the family. How you listen is equally as important as how much you talk. Strong families reassure each other by investing value in what each member shares in the family conversations.

Strong families share common goals and values. "The family that prays together stays together" has proven to be more than an adage. A sense of unity in the home can be measured by the degree to which members of the family share recreational, social, spiritual and value goals. The symbols of family sharing may be the activities in which we participate but should also include the experiences of our daily actions and living. How long has it been since your family talked about what's most important to each of you? Perhaps it starts with the question, what values do we really share? In what ways do we communicate that to each other?

Strong families do things together. They enjoy spending time in joint activities and give these priority over other outside and individual interests. They feel good about being together. That loyalty and commitment does not devalue other individual interests and proves to be a vital daily satisfaction. Each member of the family will not equally enjoy all the activities on every occasion, but being together in the shared time becomes a value in itself.

Check your family out to see if these ingredients are present. If not, become a one person change agent to shape your own family in the right direction. The International Family Foundation, Inc. believes we can change the world through families. In fact, the family is man's best hope for unity in the world. You, too, can touch the world, one family at a time. Start with yours today!

Your Children's Roots and Wings

THE ULTIMATE GIFTS FOR YOUR CHILDREN

A wise man once wrote: "There is no success that compensates for failure in the home." Over the years I have listened to many parents who have bemoaned their failures with their children even though they enjoyed extreme success in business or in other endeavors. How should we measure success or failure in our homes?

You will know that you are a success when your children are able to leave you and build an independent life of their own. We don't ever sever relationships with our children, but it is our responsibility to cut the emotional umbilical cord so that they can truly grow. A parent who dominates or intimidates to be in control of his child robs him of emotional maturity.

Let me suggest that put in its simplest terms our children need only two gifts from us: **roots and wings.** Our children grow best in the soil of security, knowing that they are loved and accepted as the persons they are. Conditional loving – the "I will love you IF you do this to please me" type – cripples the sinews of emotional muscle and produces an insecure child. He will spend his energy not only trying to win the approval of his parent but of other people as well. Unfortunately, he will never be able to please the parent and all the others. He will grow up wondering about his worth and his capabilities, struggling to "find" himself.

Family "roots" of love, understanding, nurture and guidance contribute to strong self-worth and confidence in discovering and expressing independence as adolescence fades into adulthood.

The second gift our children need from us is wings! Roots seem easier to give but wings, while more difficult, may be far more important. Just like baby eaglets are born to fly, our children are born to leave us at some point. Some of the struggles of adolescence strain the process. One day these "children" are so dependent, but the next they fly with their new wings of independence. On occasion their new independence can strike like a sword of accusation or disapproval. If we can recognize those moments as part of the natural separation process and not feel threatened by what may appear to be loss of respect, both the parent and the child will struggle through the passage into maturity more easily.

This emotional "tug of war" can feel as though the fabric of the relationship is being torn apart, but when the new "adult friends" that once were our children thank us for their "roots" while we watch them soar on their "wings", the rewards will be obvious.

Wherever you are in the process, a parent who no longer has a child would gladly trade places with you. If you are a brilliant teenager and you can flap your wings as you fly out of the nest, be grateful for the parents who let you mature in the roots of their love. The family is the foundation of our society. Let's make sure we succeed in our most important task!

The Lost Art of Reading

MAKING BOOKS IMPORTANT
TO OUR CHILDREN

Reflecting on my childhood recently, I remembered a story my grandmother told me often. Apparently, my grandfather was busy reading the newspaper and ignored my repeated requests for him to read to me. After a couple of "not now, Jimmy" responses, I grabbed a toy baseball bat and hit him over the head. "Now I guess you'll read to me, Old Man (my grandmother's favorite name for him.)"

I'm not recommending that behavior to any child, but it did recall for me that reading and books were a very important part of my childhood. Long before I went to school I had read through an illustrated comic book of the Bible. It began sitting in my grandfather's lap while he read his Bible, usually out loud. He would insert my name in special verses like John 3:16, "For God so loved Jimmy..." are words I remember in his Southern tones.

I have no doubt that my love for books, and the Bible, in particular, resulted from those early experiences. I'm reading several books now. I was disappointed to read recent research that the average adult reads two books or less a year. I don't think the computer or the telephone feeds the same joy as reading a good book.

I remember the fun of reading both to my children and my grandchildren. We read some stories often enough that they would correct me when I did not read the entire story or missed a favorite part in an effort to get them to sleep earlier. As they have grown older, they no longer need me to read to them but they still read.

Parents have an opportunity to shape the habits and values of their children—even their grandchildren—by the activities we share together. Have you had the joy of reading a book to your children? If your children are young, take advantage of reading a children's book to them. Our county is blessed with a wonderful library system and you can have a classic downloaded on your electronic reader. As our children mature, we can read the same book and discuss it.

Television and the Internet have added dimensions to our lives that can be very beneficial and productive, but a good book stimulates your imagination. Effective writing goes beyond just information! Good books are like good friends—you enjoy having them around!

Happy reading!

Lessons a Child Learns at Home

WHO WILL TEACH MY CHILDREN?

In my book, *The Family Touch*, one section deals with life situations we all face. It's called Ten Lessons Every Child Should Learn at Home. I can't cover them all in this article but there are four I want to highlight. When conflicts occur, parents will often defend their children no matter what. The lesson the child learns is that he is always right. That can be crippling in his adult life. Parents have other options. Here are some suggestions to teach your children when life presents conflict.

First, treat others with respect and honesty.

The greatest of teachers said, "Do unto others as you would have them do unto you." Some teenage girls struggle for popularity by gossiping about other girls. A child's psyche can be deeply wounded by denigrating and unnecessarily negative comments. At worst it becomes bullying and can even lead to suicidal thoughts and attempts. This is where the parents need to model behavior for the child to follow. If I fail to treat others with respect and honesty, my child will not learn this principle.

Second, learn to negotiate fairly, not just to win.

Rarely is a dispute resolved in one direction. Compromise is the art of learning how to get what you want while letting the other person get some of what he wants. Sometimes that requires meeting in the middle. Children can learn this art by acting out how to share toys or by having them take small steps toward each other from a distance until they can reach out to touch each other. Fair negotiations are not total surrenders. I must learn to listen as much as I talk when there is a disagreement. I cannot reason with an opponent in a dispute unless I fully understand his position. To listen to my child's ideas or objections allows me the position of fully explaining the differences between us and how we can reach a compromise. Only a parent who can admit a mistake will teach a child how to negotiate fairly.

Third, honor your commitments, even if it costs you.

We live in a world where honor has very little meaning. Some of us grew up hearing, "A man's word is as good as his bond." I watched my father shake hands with a customer, order a car equipped the way they discussed and wait for a check until the car was delivered. If the customer, usually by then a friend, did not remember something, after listening my Dad almost always worked out a solution. He believed his word was the most important thing he could give.

I watched the face of a child whose father had promised something. When it was obvious that the parent's commitment would not be materialized, the child's face contorted and through the tears, he said, "But you promised ..." It was a moment that the father would probably never forget. His child lost faith in his promises. Sometimes a principle, such as keeping our promises, can cost us a position, a promotion, a friendship or even finances. Each of us must decide what the price of his integrity is. Every child will know if he has an honorable parent!

Fourth, don't deceive the face in the mirror—you'll have to look at it every day of your life!

No child ever learned a more important lesson. If we deceive ourselves, deep within we know the truth. The authentic parent models for his child that special integrity which allows the child to feel secure. If the parent deceives the child, his actions will clang so loudly his words will go unheard. Each of us can check ourselves by our reflections in the mirror. A parent who says, "Don't do that …" to a child but then fails to be consistent in his own actions, practices self-deception. There is no greater deception! We bear great responsibility to teach our children by living our principles.

It occurs to me that some of these principles can work for us "older" children when we face conflicts or disputes in our churches, clubs, or community organizations, especially those involving volunteers. Think about that!

Leaving a Caring Legacy

BUILDING A BRIDGE FOR THOSE
WHO FOLLOW

When I was in college I read a poem I've never forgotten. It was called "Building the Bridge for Him." W.A. Dromgoole captured a life purpose all of us could adopt. He wrote:

An old man, traveling a lone highway,
came at evening
cold and gray, to a chasm deep and wide.
The old man crossed in the twilight dim,
for the sullen stream held no fears for him.

But he turned when he reached the other side,
And builded a bridge to span the tide.

"Old man," said a fellow pilgrim near,
"You are wasting your strength with building here;
Your journey will end with the ending day, and
You never again will pass this way.

You have crossed the chasm deep and wide.
Why build you a bridge at eventide?"

And the builder raised his old gray head:
"Good friend, on the path I have come,"
he said,
"There followed after me today a youth
Whose feet will pass this way.

"This stream, which has been as naught to me,
To that fair-haired boy may a pitfall be.
He too, must cross in the twilight dim—
Good friend, I'm building this bridge for him."

This past week as I spoke to teachers, bus drivers and administrators about our children returning for another school year, I was aware that some are just doing a job, earning a salary or trying a new career. I met some – like this bridge builder – who have a different vision of their tasks. They are building bridges for the future leaders of our county, state and nation.

When the career path you've chosen comes to the last stop sign before your parking spot, how will you evaluate why you've done what you've done. A reporter interviewed three men at a construction site with the same question, "What are you doing?" The first man said, "I'm pouring concrete." The second one answered, "I'm earning a living." The final worker raised up tall and responded, "I'm building a great cathedral."

Plato said that the unexamined life was not worth living. What are you doing today? Do you have an eye on the future and the impact you have on those who follow?

The Terrible Silence of the Decent

FREEDOM FROM FEAR

My first clue was, "They said on television that it's OK to tell." She had never spoken to a therapist before and she struggled to unburden her heart. The tears began to drip from her cheeks onto the silk blouse she wore. Years of holding a secret deep within her were being washed away. During her teen years she had been molested by her father and later by an uncle. When she told her mother and her aunt what had happened they refused to take any action. To escape from home, she married very early, but the pain of the past caused her difficulty in her relationship.

She began a process of liberation from horrible memories as the minutes rolled by. As I think of her now and the progress she has made, I wonder about her mother and her aunt. I'm sure they were decent women. Why would they choose to remain silent in the face of such abuse?

What bothers me now is the fact that many families may still participate in the terrible silence of the decent. Too often we hear the caution, "Don't get involved." We excuse ourselves sometimes by musing, "someone ought to do something about that ..." but we don't become the "someone" who does! The greatest of teachers once said, "Treat others the way you wish to be treated." Perhaps for parents we should hear treat other children the way you would want your children to be treated. Or, further, treat one in trouble the way you wish to be treated. That commandment cannot leave us in silence.

The test of a family's character is revealed in how we deal with the unexpected. No fear of embarrassment should shame us into silence when it comes to protecting our own children. That trait should also bring out our best in rescuing any child who turns to us for help.

Seeing any child in trouble or being abused calls for risk on the part of a mature adult. Appropriate interventions will certainly help that child's emotional future and may even save his or her life. We need not only to protect our children at home but also to develop a network of concern in our neighborhood by sharing with other parents and linking with helping agencies in our communities. The test of a community's character is whether we remain silent in the face of crucial issues. Think about it; let's not be caught in the web of decent silence.

Marriage:
A Happiness Factor

February was described as the month for lovers. All of us want to be loved, but that has many meanings. Infatuation, an emotional attachment, or an exhilarating feeling can be described as love. But the most satisfying love experience comes through a lasting relationship. That's why friends are so important to us. It also explains the value of marriage for many of us.

A Pew Research Center report suggests that married people are **happier** than single people. About 43 per cent of married men and women described themselves as "very happy" while only 24 per cent of unmarried men and women said the same.

The happy halo isn't the result of having children—those without children were just as likely to be happy as those without. Researchers say there seems to be something about marriage itself that boosts both men's and women's feelings of well-being. "Married people are less depressed and less lonely than their single counterparts," says University of Chicago sociologist Linda Waite. It's harder to be lonely when you've got someone to come home to every night. According to Waite, men benefit more than women from having a life-long companion. (I wasn't even in the study!)

Most women tend to talk to *everybody* while men rely on their wives as their main confidant. In addition women – usually the social planners—ensure that men stay connected to their family and friends. That's another happiness factor. Even though some might call it "nagging," married women are more likely to have husbands who drink less, smoke less, eat better, get more sleep and engage in less risky behavior than unmarried peers. Since health is linked to happiness – they are happier too.

People in the South are more likely to be married – and earlier—according to Waite's study. Having been married to a girl from the West for more than 65 years, I doubt that the geography plays as much a part as the family model in which men and women grow up.
One caution – marriage *alone* will not make one happy, but a good marriage will certainly help. Here are some tips for making it good.

1. **Good marriages are honest.**

   It's not the "golden commandment" – "thou shalt not have secrets!" It's the result of wanting to share the most important things with each other. Do you remember what your courtship was like – you could talk for hours about "nothing." Communication is the result of wanting to spend time with each other and sharing what's in your heart and mind. A good marriage is made of a good talker and a good listener – each knowing how to change places frequently!

2. **Good marriages share the important stuff.**

   I don't think your mate has to know everything you think. He or she does need to know what's most important to you. Happy mates share their dreams, hopes, faith and fears. They don't have to solve each other's problems, but being there makes it easier for each of them to tackle tough issues. When they need to, they can find help in carrying the burden. They always find their joys enlarged because they can share them with each other. They divide the burden and share the laughter!

3. **Good marriages are partnerships.**

Successful corporations merge their assets, but successful marriages pool their potential. A happily married man is more than he was when he was single because he has the confidence and support of his wife. A woman who is cherished in marriage is fulfilled in a way singleness can't touch. Together they are more than the sum of their parts.

But the partnership is always improved when they have a connection to the ultimate Source of life. God dreamed this thing called marriage before we did, and He can direct it to its highest satisfaction if we allow it. He's the ultimate Partner we need and the one to Whom both of us can surrender.

I don't ask for agreement—just thoughtful consideration. If you disagree, tell each other why; that way it will do the most good!

Marriage: A Personal Choice

It was almost a universal opening line, something nearly every person who came for marriage counseling, had in mind. Could you guess it? You probably couldn't but these three words were the underlying assumption: fix my spouse!

That's right! About 90% of the 7000 plus couples I saw in the counseling office believe their marriages would be better if only their partners would improve. Not all of them acknowledged this desire immediately; some just wanted to vent their anger.

But the most important lesson to be learned is this: if my marriage is going to improve, it's up to me! Despite our hidden hopes, none of us can really change another person. I can only change me, but I can change our relationship by making different input. Here are three important questions for every husband and wife to answer.

First, what change could I make that would improve my relationship?

Most of us know what the "hot buttons" are in our conversations. Can I make some changes in the way I relate to my spouse? Here's an example. Instead of beginning a conversation with, "You never...(fill in the blank)"; try "I wonder if...or "I would appreciate..."

What happens? I change my approach to the issue, illustrated by simply beginning my sentences with the word "I" rather than "you." The more I demonstrate that I take the responsibility for my thoughts, feelings, words and actions, the less likely I am to blame you. That's change.

Second, am I really listening to my spouse?

Too many of us assume we know what our spouses think and don't really listen to what they say. The result is that we see their lips moving, not really hearing the words, but only thinking of what we want to say when they finally stop. I'll never forget a wife who got angry as her husband apologized, because she wasn't really listening to what he said. I had listened and repeated to her what I heard him say. "He didn't say that!" What she needed to acknowledge was that she didn't hear it!

Try reflecting, "If I heard you right, what you said was…" Once you have agreed, then you can respond. Too often we remain angry at what we thought we heard rather than what was actually spoken.

Third, is this the way I want to expend my energy in the marriage?

Some time ago I asked a husband what his goal for his marriage was. He said quickly, "I want to be happy with her." When I asked if what he was doing would accomplish that goal, he admitted it would not. Each of us must examine our behavior. Is what you are doing moving you and your spouse toward your goal?

Insanity may have been well defined as "doing the same thing over and over but expecting a different result." If my best energy is spent in winning arguments, will I accomplish the closeness I say I want? What other choices could I make?

Marriage is, at its best, a personal choice.

The choice is to be the best partner I can be. Far too many couples I have known have resigned themselves to living with their spouses, because they have no other choice. The happiest couples I have known have learned to say: I don't have to live with you, but I choose to live with you. Think about that!

Marriage: Keys to Success

This year Ruth and I have been married for 65 years. When my granddaughter married, I was asked what the key to a lasting marriage was. I wrote an entire book, *TRY MARRIAGE BEFORE DIVORCE.* I have developed these three for a briefer response.

Every marriage needs a gift.

Specials gifts, purchased or produced from one's talents, are important in relationships. Remembering anniversaries, birthdays, and other special occasions would be included in this concept. But the most meaningful gifts are the special "I love you" gifts that come without an occasion. They simply say "I love you."

In marriage, the most significant gift anyone can give is the gift of self. How do we do that? It begins with attention – the focused listening with intent to understand what your beloved is feeling and saying.

Often that discovery comes through non-verbal associations rather than the words that are spoken. The single most often expressed complaint in marriage counseling has to do with being taken for granted or ignored. Unfaithfulness often begins not with sexual attraction but with someone paying attention to a lonely or neglected spouse.

A major foundation for a lasting relationship is learning to give of yourself to your spouse – attentively, emotionally, psychologically, physically and spirituality.

Every marriage needs a goal.

At its best love is not two people standing eyeball to eyeball lost in each other's gaze. Instead it is two people standing shoulder to shoulder looking ahead together. Companionship is the sharing of mutual interests and pursuits that draw people to each other. Single people will often ask where to look for a potential mate. I do not suggest bars (unless you simply want to make sure that he or she drinks). It makes so much more sense to pay attention to the activities you enjoy and see who shares your interest in church, politics, reading or sports.

Developing a common goal requires conversation, exchanging ideas, and views in a non-judgmental way. Some of us have become competitive rather than compassionate when it comes to goals. We may "win" the immediate discussion but lose the ultimate direction. The Hebrew prophet asked a penetrating question, "How can two walk together unless they are agreed?"

Every marriage needs a God!

Marriages where couples share faith and prayer have an additional resource for the tests of life. A number of years ago, when the divorce rate was one in two marriages, statistics reflected that couples who regularly worshiped with each other had an astounding divorce rate of one in one hundred forty-five marriages!

The cliché' "The couple that prays together stays together" is not fiction.

A young couple sat in my counseling office and we grieved together the loss of their infant child. On one occasion, as they prepared to leave, the husband said to me, "I don't know how any couple survives this kind of loss alone. We would not have made it without knowing God was there."

Marriage is a life-long covenant, but it can only be fulfilling if these truths are practiced by both partners. No one marries a perfect spouse. As my friend, Billy Graham's wife, Ruth, once wisely said: "Marriage is made up of two good forgivers." A true friend is someone who knows you the way you are and loves you anyway.

Happy is the person who is married to his or her best friend!

TRANSFORMING THE MUNDANE TO THE MAGNIFICENT

Where is God when I Need Him?

I'M NEVER ALONE

Probably the most difficult and intriguing question we ever ask begins, why?

An investigator has many questions—what, who, when, where and even how before the why question is asked. Facts build the foundation for asking about motive; that's the why question.

A parent can often make the mistake of starting with the why question before assembling the factual information. Therapists are trained not to ask why. When we think about it, why questions are the most interrogating ones we are ever asked. When faced with that question, the child often withdraws and fails to respond.

As a pastor and as a therapist I have often been asked, why did God allow this? In fact, there are a lot of questions we throw at God – Why this? Why now? Why me? The truth is that most of those cannot or will not be answered.

Although when we probe deeply into ourselves, we may discover that the answers are hidden within us. "Why this" can often be uncovered when I examine my behavior and find a root cause for the struggle that seems to defeat me at every turn. I may find a habit that tends to debilitate me. I may identify a cause for my behavior based on a fear of being exposed or facing a challenge I am not ready to handle.

The "why now" questions also offer some insight when we check our calendars and discover patterns of behavior that belie our protests about the unfairness of life. The "why me" are often based on our willingness to hide behind our being "victimized" by life and dealing with it by avoiding all personal responsibilities.

Sometimes we discover that we have made God over in our image and likeness. Who determined for any of us that God is fair?

Too often we want everything to be equaled out. The most ineffective player on the team is to be rewarded equally with the one whose input helps to make the team achieve!

The Bible spends more time reminding us of God's justice than of His love. *It is not BECAUSE we have sinned that God loves us. It is in fact, IN SPITE OF our sinning that He loves us.* None of us can truly claim a righteousness God demands. When you reach the bottom line of our questions, the only one we can ask that makes any sense is, why does He love me so?

In the answer to that question I discover that God is always there no matter what my need may be!

Get Out of the Dumpster

DISCOVERING FREEDOM

Have you ever felt like you were living in a trash heap? Before I retired I listened to a man who complained bitterly about almost everything in his life. His view was such that he had to look up to see bottom. He felt life had passed him by and there was no hope for a better future. Dumpster living does not have much hope. Here are some steps to help you get out of your dumpster.

First, to borrow a word from Jesus, "Let the past bury its dead!" (Matthew 8:22, KJV) Too many folks I've met are losing their choices in the present because **they are dominated by some mistakes of the past.**

A young woman had just given birth to her first child, but when I spoke with her the guilt over a previous abortion had almost robbed her of the joy that should have filled her heart. Once a word has been spoken, it can't be taken back. Perhaps an apology, a request for forgiveness and action that shows a different view can remedy the situation, but that word still exists.

Of all the teachings of the Christian faith, forgiveness must bring the greatest joy to the heart of the sinner! **To have the past removed is renewing.** The Psalmist praised God when he said, "Who forgives all your iniquities." (Psalm 103:3, KJV) All we must do is accept His forgiveness, forgive ourselves and move away from the guilt of the past.

Another way we often hold on to the past is by **blaming someone else for what happened.** To hold on to a grudge is like keeping a chain around your own body. We cannot be truly free until we release the bitterness that lingers in our blaming.

To gain freedom from the past I need to accept my responsibility for the ways I have failed and discover a new goal which can become the course of my aspirations and actions. In fact, the foundation of change is expressed in forgetting what lies behind and pressing on to the goal of a new prize. There we discover motivation for release from the past, new hope for the future and direction to accomplish it.

Unless you like the smell of trash, a dumpster is no place to live! **Today is the day to get out of yours.**

The Ears of the Heart

CAN YOU HEAR THE SONG?

Near the end of the musical, "Les Misérables," a moving theme begins and builds. It asks the question, "Can you hear the people sing?" The chorus joins the soloist for a stirring ending. People are often on their feet applauding at the end of the performance.

Music has a way of lifting our spirits and putting melodies in our hearts. I still get a lump in my throat and pride in my heart when the national anthem is played. As we think back about the sacrifices so many have made that allow us to worship, to speak or even to protest in a free country, we are grateful. In a way the music of the nation carries the dream we have for a better future.

A similar experience often happens in the music we hear or listen to on our various devices. Some years ago, I was traveling with a singing group and one line impressed me as the soloist sang: "Anyone can sing when the sun is shining bright, but you need a song in your heart at night!"

Do you have a song that carries you through the lonely nights of life? For many of us the words of hymns resonate in our minds and encourage us when we are down. George Beverly Shea's singing of "How Great Thou Art" often floods my mind when I remember attending Billy Graham's crusades here in Atlanta. Martin Luther's great hymn "A Mighty Fortress is our God" reminds us that the victory has been won for us; we know the outcome of history.

Listening to so many patients through the years, the most persistent memory of their mental song is one of defeat and discouragement. Let me suggest a way to hear the song in your spirit.

First, **memorize** some verses of Scripture that you can recall when tests of life be-fuddle you. James' advice is to "Draw nigh to God, and he will draw nigh to you." (James 4:8, KJV) David reassured himself with the reminder "The Lord is my Shepherd; I shall not want." (Psalm 23:2, KJV) Or Jesus' blessing: "Let not your heart be troubled, neither let it be afraid." (John 14:27, KJV)

Let those positive thoughts repeat themselves in your mind to create a calmness, even amid your emotional storm. You may not be a singer but try reminding yourself of songs that affirm God's presence and work in your life. "Our God is an awesome God" and "The joy of the Lord is my strength" are words to uplift the mind and energize the spirit.

It's true that it's often darkest just before dawn, but having a positive, uplifting song in your heart can bring the bright sunshine of hope. The reassuring Psalm says, "The entrance of thy words gives light; it gives understanding unto the simple." (Psalm 119:130, KJV)

Let the soul's sunshine in; it will chase the darkness of the mind away!

Love Prints on the Heart

WHERE DO YOU ENGRAVE?

Henry W. Longfellow wrote a great line, "Lives of great men all remind us, we may make our lives sublime, and departing, leave behind us, footprints on the sands of time." While it is an inspiring goal, not many of us expect to leave that kind of mark on history. Yet, Thomas Carlyle once defined history as the "study of the lives of great men." But few of us think in terms of our greatness. Most of us simply go through life without thinking about our influence on others. All of us do leave prints in our world. The science of finger-printing often uncovers evidence that leads to the conviction of a crime. Even the more recent scientific study of our DNA can uncover sources of our personal journey and ancestry.

But perhaps the most imprint prints we leave behind are heart prints. I recently read a description of "good works of the heart," simply called "heart prints." The simple question all of us face as we journey through our lives is: what kind of prints are you leaving behind? We may have no choice about our finger prints or our foot prints, but we can make choices about our heart prints. Thoughtfully choose where you want to leave a heart print today.

A random act of kindness may be one form of a heart print. The best heart prints are those we choose to share with others. It may be a deliberate compliment, "I admire you." "I appreciate your influence or service in our community." "Thank you for your service to our country" is one more frequently shared with active and retired military. "You did a fine job" may be an indelible heart print for a child who is seldom praised at home. Affirmations of one's value or appreciation of a service rendered are other examples.

Don't wait for a special occasion. **Find someone today and give them the gift of one of your heart prints.** Someone's world may be changed because you placed a heart print with him. It may also change your life!

Age is Just a Number

ANTICIPATION FOR MORE

This past week I had a birthday. I don't feel 86, but a good friend in California just died at 90. One of my other friends sent a message: "Death is the number one killer in humans!" What a *joy* he was on that day.

It has caused me to reflect on aging just a bit. With the television accusations about President Trump going on, I thought back over fourteen presidents who have served during my lifetime. One of my "bucket" list items was to visit all the Presidential libraries. I completed those visits several years ago and thought back about the history of our nation under each of the leaders we elected.

After living more than eight decades I have asked myself what I'm leaving behind as a legacy of my life. Obviously, the most important contributions to the world that Ruth and I share are our three children, four grandchildren and three great grandchildren. We have been blessed immensely.

In more than sixty-four years in the ministry I have been blessed to serve several congregations, one for more than a quarter of a century. In those associations I remember the members of congregations, people I've baptized and those I nurtured in the faith. Watching them grow in grace is one of the great rewards any minister ever shares.

The more than fifty-five years I spent in the counseling office, much of it concurrent with the pastoral years, have brought wonderful people into my life. Sometimes we met under difficult circumstances but those who reaffirmed their marriage and family values remain good friends and positive relationships. On holidays I often get cards or messages about the progress they've made in their lives. If you haven't guessed it already, I've learned that relationships are the *greatest rewards* of living. Some are built-ins. I was blessed with great grandparents on both my Father and my Mother's side of the family. Because my mother was still a teenager when I was born, I spent many important hours with my grandparents and learned so many lessons I never want to forget. I'm sure I didn't understand everything they tried to teach me in those early years, but most have been invaluable guides to my life-long relationships.

My parents exposed me to some really important influences in my life, beyond my grandparents, aunts and uncles and some great cousins. Many Sundays after church we sat at the lunch table with the guest speakers who visited our churches. They were among the "great" names of the evangelical world. I was introduced to a world of ideas and needs that expanded my horizons for my adult life.

As strange as it may sound, I'm grateful for the tough times of my life. I've learned that grief and moments of struggle make you bitter or better. Because good people surrounded me in the "trials" of my life, I learned the joy of giving back to those in need around me. I trust that I will have many more years to complete that task.

Even if it is a large number, eighty-six is just a number. I look forward to packing more opportunities for God's blessings into the years ahead. In God we trust is not just a national motto, I've learned that it is the only way to live happily.

Life After Death

THINKING ABOUT ETERNITY

On Sundays I teach a class of adults called the Pathfinders. They can ask some questions that are very difficult to answer, but the questions children ask are far more demanding. A child whose father had died asked me, "Is my Daddy in heaven?" Tough question.

The child was not old enough to understand theology. I knew some Bible passages I could share with her. I decided instead to ask her what she really wanted to know. Imagine my surprise when she told me she had overheard her Grandpa say, "I hope he burns in hell." But her Grandma said, "You shut up!" She looked at me with pleading eyes and asked, "Did my Daddy go to hell because he shot himself?" Now the issue was very clear.

My answer was, "Sometimes people say things when they hurt or are angry that are not true. I don't know why your Grandpa said what he did, but I do know that your Daddy believed he was going to heaven. I was there when he was baptized and said he believed in Jesus. Do you remember that?" She softly cried and whimpered, "Yes."

What to say next seems very difficult. "I believe that Jesus promised to all who believe in Him a place in what He called, 'My Father's house.' I heard your Daddy say, 'I believe in Jesus.' I think Jesus heard that and I believe He will keep His promises, do you?" She nodded her head quietly.

For me **the simplest theology is faith in what God has done and what He promised to do**. I couldn't tell her all about eternity because I don't know that. But even at her tender age we shared something together – we both believed Jesus would keep His promises.

Our conversation went on for a bit. But I learned two things from her question.

First, **I need to make sure what the question being asked really is before I try to give an answer**, especially to a child.

Second, she needed to hear a **loving word about her daddy more than a theological response.**

Life after death is really important but life BEFORE death is more important at times. Sharing with our children what we believe and why we believe it is the key to fulfilling parenthood.

How are you answering the questions your children ask you? Think about it.

One Day Masterpiece

One of the many skills my wife has is sewing prayer quilts for our church's ministry to those in need. They are placed on the altar and members pray for that need and tie a knot to symbolize their prayer. The quilt is delivered to the person for whom it was requested. Often they run their fingers over the knots as they cover themselves in this special quilt.

It reminded me of a placemat my mother brought home from a restaurant, The quote printed on the mat said, **"Live one day at a time, and make it a masterpiece."** A simple gesture like a knot in a prayer quilt, a note written to a friend struggling with illness or grief, or an email that says "I'm thinking of you today" may be part of your masterpiece day.

All of us have too many ordinary days and too few masterpiece days in our lives.

I start a lot of days with good intentions and many of them remain unfulfilled at the close of the hours I have.

But I have some days that fall into the "masterpiece" category. A surprise phone call where I heard the need in the voice of the caller, listened and prayed with that person, although we were miles away from each other. In the process of a day I discover that:

A masterpiece day is made up of many minutes. We can waste a few without losing a whole day. Don't judge yourself too harshly if you blow an opportunity to be helpful to a friend. Another moment for masterpiece living will come up soon enough if we are aware. I can apologize for a failed effort and get a fresh start. That's one of the beautiful experiences of life – failure is never final unless I allow it to be. Life is full of moments where we can use the "eraser" of a fresh start if we are willing to swallow our pride and ask for forgiveness.

A masterpiece day can be experienced after a poor start. In therapy changes occur when a person can find a new frame of reference—a different way of seeing things. A wise man wrote "Discovery is seeing what other people see and finding a new way to describe it." Today is the first day of the rest of your life! That is more than a simple fact; it is a statement of reframing reality. Being willing to accept a period at the end of yesterday's unfulfilling efforts and staring fresh to work on today's opportunities provides a reset. All of us need one of those from time to time.

A masterpiece day rises above our self-criticism levels and allows us to see new vistas of opportunity for fulfillment. Pessimism lives in our willingness to accept the things around us as though they cannot be changed. Oliver W. Holmes got it right when he said: "Some men see things the way they are, and ask why. I see things the way they could be and ask why not?" Masterpiece living is discovered in those "why not" questions in our lives. **Make today one of those!**

The Measure of Life

THE PARADOX OF POSSESSION

Some teachings of Jesus seem very hard to live by.

For instance, He said "For whosoever will save his life shall lose it; but whosoever loses his life for my sake and the gospel's, the same shall save it. For what shall it profit a man if he shall gain the whole world, and lose his own soul?" (Mark 8:35-36, KJV)

Some years ago, a very wealthy man sat in my office and told me about his level of unhappiness. He could have bought anything he wanted but had learned that nothing he bought could bring him real peace and satisfaction. "I'm just a walking checkbook to my family, and I am never really sure what my 'friends' want from me. Do you know what I mean?" I thought about the words of Jesus as he protested the availability of money.

In 1957 I was invited to New York as a part of the Billy Graham Madison Square Garden team. An unusual set of circumstances took me to the home of another very wealthy couple who had heard Dr. Graham on television. Their penthouse suite overlooked Central Park. But this couple were not complaining about their wealth; they simply acknowledged their thirst for some spiritual direction. As we prayed together, each of them received Christ into their lives. They "lost" their trust in physical assets and found a spiritual foundation. It was a moment I'll never forget.

This was a principle I wrote about in my book, *Getting More Family out of Your Dollar.* Among the lessons about money and family is this one:

More family is not necessarily the result of more money!

Many of us can look back on times when we had a lot fewer material goods, but we enjoyed our relationships and treasured our friendships. Later when we had more things in our lives, we discovered that each of them could bring more responsibilities. Sometimes those responsibilities became burdens.

A good friend of mine shared this life lesson: **a man cannot be free of what he possesses until he learns to give it away!**

It raises a question for each of us to ponder: do I possess things or do they in some way control me? When what we possess drives us, we miss the most important values in life—the unseen or spiritual realities.

A wise man is the one who has learned to use things and bless people with them. The saddest of men are those who use people to bless themselves. Let me suggest that today you try three things:

One, **express an attitude of gratitude for a resources in life that you have gained.** A simple sentence that begins, "I am thankful today for..." requires some thought to fill in the blank.

Second, **try giving a bit of yourself away.** A simple greeting to someone you see on the street, in a shop or in a social setting may offer a lift of encouragement. If you see someone without a smile, give him one of yours!

Third, **invest some of your resources in a cause or service to help others.** David Green, the founder of Hobby Lobby, has recently written a book entitled, *Giving it ALL Away and Getting it ALL back Again.* In it he reveals a basic principle of life: God owns everything, but He allows us to manage it for Him. The Bible defines stewardship in that way: handling the resources with which you've been entrusted as a careful manager of what belongs to Someone else.

Jesus' question still stands: what profit is there in gaining the whole world if, in the process, you lose your soul? Think about that.

Don't Quit Living Yet

STAY ALIVE ALL YOUR LIFE

I was asked to speak to a group of seniors about planning and enjoying retirement. My subject—Stay Alive ALL Your Life—seemed amusing at first, but I recalled for them that in almost every family there is a person who is existing but really is "dead" or perhaps "deadbeat" to the other family members.

The actor, George Burns, was asked the secret of his youthful attitude. His response was, "Don't fall in love with your bed."

Being alive is more than just breathing through another day. It is an attitude of expectancy about living, an eagerness for what is next. The person who merely makes it through another day usually misses most, if not, all of the excitement of the day.

Here's a plan for making your day better. A little girl was told by her grandmother, "You are like a butterfly. You fly from plant to plant and leave a little beauty everywhere you stop." What a wonderful way of saying, "Be contagious." *Happy people create happy surroundings,* adding value to the lives of those around us. Each of us spreads our influence on others in each day's activities.

Staying alive all through your life results from these three steps:

1. Determining your priorities,
2. giving yourself away and
3. appreciating life.

First, to prioritize is simply to **decide what's important to you** and to concentrate on doing it. No one can decide for you what your priorities are! Frustrated people think everything is important. They fail to highlight the essential and then add other possibilities.

As a part of what's important, **try sharing yourself with someone else every day.** It is true that the only love we keep is the love we give away. Give an unexpected compliment, write a thoughtful note, or discover a generous act which will brighten someone else's day immensely. Think of yourself as a supplier of other's needs rather than a drain on their resources. Your attitude will get different responses.

Each of us has the capacity to **express appreciation for something every day.** A friend of mine runs a Chick-fil-A restaurant. He reminds his employees that they are in the business of sharing uncommon kindness, not just serving food. It shows in every server.

Without being phony you can enrich your days by sharing appreciation with someone each day. I want to live like that; don't you? It's called **living without limits!**

CONCLUSION

Pilate was troubled after writing the sentence to describe the crime that had Jesus crucified. He was challenged by Jewish leaders about the identification over the cross which read, "This is Jesus, the King of the Jews." I don't know why Pilate wrote that. Perhaps he was confessing his own faith. He may have been mocking those who had intimidated him into capitulating over the sentence to kill Jesus. We'll never fully know. We only know what he replied: "What I have written, I have written."

I have shared over my lifetime with the people who are important to me as a pastor, a teacher, a therapist, and a writer. I understand something of what Pilate must have felt. What I have written, I have written too. I hope you have been entertained, stimulated, dug into the mastery and imagined the mystery of your own thoughts through what I have written.

I welcome your response.

My email address is jekiff@hotmail.com

ABOUT THE AUTHOR

Dr. James Kilgore is a licensed family therapist, minister, bestselling author, and international speaker with over 55 years of experience. He has earned doctorates in pastoral counseling and psychology, as well as post-doctoral certification in marriage and family therapy. Born in Georgia, he has lived in California, Florida, Minnesota, and South Carolina before returning to the Peach State.

Throughout the years, Dr. Kilgore was appointed by the former governor of Georgia, George Busbee, as the first chairman of the Georgia Marriage and Family Counseling Licensing Board. He founded Atlanta's Northside Counseling Center in 1969, and since 1975 he has traveled internationally in the role of President of the International Family Foundation, Inc. He and his wife, Mrs. Kilgore, founded Lake Arrowhead Chapel in Cherokee County, Georgia, in 1980, where he served as pastor for more than twenty-three years.

Escaping Anxiety is his landmark 16th book, coming just in time to help scores of people whose anxiety originated with or was heightened by the pandemic, social distancing measures, and other unpredictable and life-changing events of the 21st century. Other popular titles include *Try Marriage Before Divorce*, *Dr. Kilgore's Feel Good Parenting Book*, *Being Up in a Down World*, and *Living Without Limits*.

Dr. and Mrs. Kilgore have been married for 65 years and had three children, four grandchildren, and three great grandchildren. A Fellow and Life Member of the American Association for Marriage and Family Therapy, Dr. Kilgore consults with family therapists in the Atlanta metropolitan area, teaches the Pathfinders class he has instructed for over two decades at Canton First Methodist, continues to speak at universities, churches, and clubs around the globe, and contributes to magazine and newspaper columns across the nation.

Made in the USA
Columbia, SC
22 November 2022